BoomerBroadcast: Baby Boomer reflects on the journey from living life in *the* Sixties to living life in *her* Sixties

BoomerBroadcast: Baby Boomer reflects on the journey from living life in *the* Sixties to living life in *her* Sixties

Lynda Davis

Published in October 2014
To Order BOOMERBROADcast:
www.amazon.com
SRP: $15.99

Dedication

To all the ones I've loved before but especially the ones I love now – my husband, George, my brother Ron Duff who earned the degree in English I wish I had, and my parents Barbara and Clayton for raising their Boomer Broad the best way they could in the amazing fifties and sixties; she didn't turn out too bad after all – despite being caught smoking behind the high school when she was twelve. Thanks to my Boomer girlfriends who have been my rod and my staff throughout my life. You all know who you are. Thanks also to Donna Kakonge for encouraging me to pull my finger out and get this book done.

Preface

Baby Boomers have led interesting lives and share a special mind-set and value system that grew from being raised by The Greatest Generation. Then, we challenged what we had learned. We took the good stuff, such as a work ethic and integrity and amped it up with the sexual revolution, questioning authority and getting ahead.

As a Beta Boomer (one of the early ones, born in 1947) and a first-born, I have found it hard to keep my mouth shut. Bossy older sister grew into bossy older boomer. I began working in the family business at the age of eight and for the next fifty years I worked part-time and full-time at various jobs, retiring at an age when I still had, hopefully, a third of my life ahead of me. One of my retirement projects was to write a book advising young women on business and life issues. So I took some writing courses, networked with other people, and then nothing happened.

Blogging was becoming more popular and initially I discounted the idea thinking I didn't want to commit to producing something I couldn't deliver. After making little progress on my book, I revisited the blogging idea and decided to give it a go. Once again, I couldn't keep my mouth shut. Ideas and material to write about suddenly exploded and I needed a receptacle for everything banging around in my head. So, *BOOMERBROADcast* is basically a brain dump.

What began as a voice for Baby Boomer women has turned out to be of interest to men and young women as well. We still have thirty years left to shake things up. Just like fifty years ago, many of us are still working and dating but we now have more time for community and political activity, traveling, taking care of ourselves and trying to squeeze the most out of every day we have.

The Women's Movement has made great strides but there's still a lot of work to do. We're still paid less than men; we're confronted with prejudices men never experience and do not entirely understand; older women are invisible to the media, and Boomers' voices are being overshadowed by divergent interests.

I hope you enjoy reading my light-hearted manifesto on how to make the world a better place for everyone, not just Boomers. These really are the best years of our lives. And we still don't really trust anyone over thirty.

Lynda Davis
www.boomerbroadcast.net

Perspective from a Future Old Broad

From the perspective of a woman in her early forties such as myself, *BoomerBroadcast: Baby Boomer reflects on the journey from living life in the Sixties to living life in her Sixties* by Lynda Davis gives me a powerful understanding of a history that shapes so much of our daily lives, a present that helps me to understand my parents' generation, as well as a strong glimpse into my own future as an old broad.

The beginning of the book takes us back into the sixties to help the reader understand what life was like during those times. The special thing about this book that even if you do recall the sixties and you are from this generation, the magical viewpoint of Lynda Davis leaves you with a one-of-kind glimpse of sixties life from Davis's perspective. Each of the nine chapters that follow the first chapter are filled with handy tips and insightful commentary on everything from people, places, mind, body and causes, business, fashion, books and media. The people and places Davis mentions are interesting, funny and her writing is electric and filled with high energy. Her chapter about the mind brings up important topics that are actually rather "hot" topics going on right now and in the future for the mental health of millions of people. Davis brings up important insights about the body and the causes she chooses to focus on are legendary and something that millions of people can relate to.

What struck me most about Davis's book was her business section by far! This section is filled with vital advice for anyone who wants to live a more profitable present and future. What Davis chooses to focus on are sometimes the handy educational knowledge and "street sense knowledge," rather that many of us did not ever receive in our school experiences. The fashion chapter is contemporary and shows that Davis has a real style sense too that is worth investing in because she mentions brands, names and fashion labels and fashion companies that are legendary and will last a long time.

Being a writer myself, Davis's book is exciting and shows that this woman is excessively well-read. Her book reviews are enjoyable to read and including this chapter makes you feel as though you have about one hundred books right in one book! The same goes with her media chapter. Filled with movie reviews and TV reviews that are geared to the boomer market, what Davis chooses to comment on will certainly be classics for my future that add to my own personal repertoire of media knowledge.

You will be happy that you chose to purchase Lynda Davis's book. This boomer broad has a lot of fantastic things to read.

Donna Kay Cindy Kakonge, BJ, MA, ABD, LLB
Author/Teacher/ Journalist/Publisher/Jill-of-all-Trades
to supplement writing ☺
http://kakonged.com

Table of Contents

Chapter 1	Remember	Those Were The Days My Friend, We Thought They'd Never End . . . Mary Hopkin, 1968
Chapter 2	People	All You Need is Love . . . The Beatles, 1967
Chapter 3	Places	Get Off Of My Cloud . . . Rolling Stones, 1966
Chapter 4	Mind	The Sounds of Silence . . . Simon & Garfunkel, 1964
Chapter 5	Body	You Make Me Feel Like a Natural Woman . . . Aretha Franklin, 1968
Chapter 6	Causes	United We Stand . . . Brotherhood of Man, 1970
Chapter 7	Business	T-T-Takin' Care of Business . . . Bachman-Turner Overdrive, 1973
Chapter 8	Fashion	Be Sure To Wear Some Flowers in Your Hair . . .Scott McKenzie, 1967
Chapter 9	Books	I want to be a Paperback Writer . . . The Beatles, 1966
Chapter 10	Media	In the year 2525 . . . Zager and Evans, 1969

Chapter 1
Nostalgia

*Those Were The Days My Friend,
We Thought They'd Never End
. . . Mary Hopkin, 1968*

Rockin' and rollin' at the hop

Picture this—1964—a high school dance. All the cute girls are dancing with their regular boyfriends. Some of the guys have broken through the line of wallflowers and asked several of the unspoken-for girls to dance. And there are several circles of dateless girls (myself included) dancing to The Beatles' *I Wanna Hold Your Hand*. The dance floor is packed and everyone's having a great time. We all know every word to every song, including the backup vocals and we don't hesitate to sing out along with the music.

With the exception of seeing a sea of grey hair and bald heads, that's exactly what it looked like at a Doo-Wop fundraiser dance put on by my friend's tennis group one Friday night earlier this year. In fact there were still quite a few teased, bleached bobs and weird perms in the crowd as we all revived our classic sixties dance moves—some better than others. We twisted, slow-danced, jived, mashed potatoes and generally did whatever felt good in time to Roy Orbison, The Nylons, The Diamonds, Del Shannon, Paul Anka, The Beach Boys, Sam Cooke and a long list of other hit-makers from the fifties and sixties.

A friend's husband (a retired fire-fighter) provided non-stop dance partner services for the single ladies for most of the slow dances as we took turns cutting in. We bopped to songs beautifully delivered by *The GoldTones*, four guys in classy white sports jackets with black shirts and pants.

I'm always amazed when I attend such events that more than fifty years have elapsed since we attended those high-school dances in the gymnacafetorium or Teen Town at the Masonic Hall. Back then, a fight might break out between some of the tougher guys having a smoke or a drink in the parking lot. But generally they were pretty tame affairs compared with the easy sex and copious supplies of booze and drugs at teen parties today.

If anyone had sex in the washroom or parking lot at this year's fundraiser dance, they'd have returned to brag about it and we'd have erected a monument to them. Today, at least, no one in our crowd has to worry about getting pregnant and resorting to the unreliable Coke douche. And we don't stay out too late anymore—can't stay awake that long. But we're still cool. We still remember the words to all the songs and have a ton of fun. A little Buddy Holly or Dion and The Belmonts and we're off. That's all it takes to temporarily wipe out fifty years.

I've become one of them

We've all been on the receiving end of laments from individuals older than ourselves about how things were *soooo* different in their day. In addition to surprising myself by now reading the editorials and op-ed pages in the daily newspaper (it's because I *care*), I'm sadly now one of those people who rolls her eyes at today's youth and moans about how it's so different from when I was young. You know how it works:

"I can't believe ten-year olds have cell phones. When I was a kid we only had one phone for fourteen people in our house – and it was a party-line shared with half a dozen neighbours." or "When I was in high school, the girls all had to wear skirts and dresses every day, with *nylons and garter belts*." or

"Our parents never drove us anywhere. We walked or rode our bikes – without helmets – or we'd never go anywhere – and my one-and-only two-wheeler was third-hand."

"I only had one winter coat and one pair of winter boots and they had to last two or three years."

My Dad made a comment the other day about how each generation's lifestyle is easier and better than the previous ones and how that's a good thing. It reminded me to stop whining about the perceived injustices and celebrate the improvements instead. Leaving home at the age of seventeen and moving to Toronto by myself to start working for a living cuts no ice with those who happily live at home free-of-charge until they're thirty. Oops – did it again. Sorry.

They really weren't the good old days – today's days are 'way better. Anyway, check out one of my favourite Monty Python skits with four Yorkshiremen talking about how they've improved their lot in life. It always makes me laugh –

http://www.youtube.com/watch?v=13JK5kChbRw.

Re-living the Glory Days

Until this week I had never heard of P.J. O'Rourke. Don't know how I could have missed him. I just finished reading his latest book called *The Baby Boom* which is an account of his life from the perspective of a Beta Boomer, like myself. Born in November 1947 in Toledo Ohio, he is now a high-profile American satirist, political journalist and writer. His reflections are funny, enlightening and so very familiar – except for all the drug use which I was never a part of. And judging from his productivity during his drug years, I'm not sorry I missed it.

O'Rourke lived the quintessential American Boomer life, growing up in a safe neighbourhood in the company of loads of other kids in the same age group. He compares the boomer habit of driving around in cars listening to car radios, going to drive-in burger joints and going "parking" during high school years as our version of Facebook, although he never actually met a car-hop on roller skates. I'm not sure if roller skates was the qualifier here or carhop. His experiences and perspectives on the sex, drugs and rock & roll generation are a great read.

On sex, he says, *"Fumbling anticipation generated a kind of prolonged bliss that fumbled completion has rarely matched."*

On drugs: *"Drugs taught a generation of Americans the metric system. And who indeed knew what a kilo or a gram was before pot and coke began arriving in those quantities."*

On rock'n'roll: One of his more interesting observations is that most of the great music loved by baby boomers was not actually the product of boomers themselves. For example, all of the Beatles were born in the early 1940s, as were all of the Stones and most of the social icons we claim as our own, such as Bob Dylan (1941), Marvin Gaye (1939), John Lennon (1940), Mick Jagger (1943), and Gloria Steinem

(1934) were pre-boomers. Elvis was born in 1935. Not one of the organizers of Woodstock was a Baby Boomer. He further qualifies the sixties timeline as actually occurring between 1967 when the Baby Boom *"had fully infested academia and coming to an abrupt halt in 1973 when conscription ended and herpes began"*.

On retirement: *"It's estimated that by 2030, when the last of our generation is struggling with how to get the Depends on after the Levitra's been taken, Boomer-Americans will be raking in Social Security and Medicare benefits costing half of all the money spent in Washington. We're riding down the highway of life in a Welfare Cadillac (with the right-turn indicator blinking for miles and miles)."*

While we cannot argue that we're going to be a huge drain on social spending, at least we can take comfort in the thought that we earned it, most of us contributing enormous taxes for forty or fifty years. Ironically it won't be our money that will be subsidizing this; it's the Gen X'ers and Y's. They'll be working their young fannies off as our money has all been spent on current political folly.

Describing the ridiculousness of so-called creativity in the sixties, O'Rourke quotes a poem by Aram Saroyan that goes as follows: *"priit"*. That's it. One word. This resonated with me because a couple of years ago I attended a writing workshop that included one such poet. He arrived late because his bicycle had a flat tire on the way over. He was sixty-something, lean, sweating, wearing a tee shirt, shorts and sandals, and was bald with a long, gray ponytail. This guy was a total holdover from the sixties hippies era who specialized in one-word poems that he said needed an understanding of the hidden mathematical connotations to be understood. Sheesh! That was taking Japanese minimalist poetry a bit too far for my liking or understanding. These people really do exist.

O'Rourke missed Woodstock because his girlfriend at the time had made a feeble gesture at committing suicide by swallowing too many Midol and One-A-Days. *"I was also slightly disappointed about missing Woodstock until the nightly news reported that it had turned into a catastrophic, drug-addled, rain-drenched disaster area lacking food, shelter, drinking water, and Porta Potties. Then I was furious about missing Woodstock."*

I'm at risk here of wanting to quote the entire book I loved it so much. Although obviously written from a purely American perspective,

Canadians can find much to relate to. We had Yorkville, Rochedale and our own hippie sixties scene. And we provided refuge to countless American draft dodgers, many of whom chose to remain in Canada even after amnesty. O'Rourke is intelligent and literate with an extensive vocabulary, and I'm looking forward to reading more of his material.

We'll miss you, Phil

Baby Boomers were sad to hear of the passing of Phil Everly, the younger of The Everly Brothers at the age of seventy-four. I had the privilege of seeing them perform three times – first in 1984 at what was then called The O'Keefe Centre in Toronto, again a couple of years later at Roy Thomson Hall and a bonus third time when they played four numbers during a surprise break in a Paul McCartney concert at Air Canada Centre in Toronto. I remember loving their perfect harmonies as they serenaded us on AM radio in the fifties and sixties. Seeing them perform "live" twenty years later only reinforced my love of their music. At The O'Keefe Centre and Roy Thomson performances, smartly attired in tuxedos, they surpassed my expectations of a live performance – still delivering perfect harmonies. We'll always be "Devoted to You."

Wait 'til the midnight hour

Wilson Pickett had big plans back in 1965 when he suggestively rocked out "In the midnight hour." He was "gonna take you girl and hold you, and do all the things I told you. . ?" Fifty years later things are a little different. I'm embarrassed to confess we may be home in bed asleep when we hit the midnight hour this New Years' Eve. Is it 2015 already?

Last year, we attended a lovely dinner and dance with a group of friends on New Year's Eve. The problem began when we paid the bill for our dinner at 10:30 p.m. and we still had ninety minutes to go until midnight. It was all we could do to manage a few dances and stay awake long enough to welcome in the New Year. At 12:01 we were outa' there like a shot. There were traffic jams in our little neighbourhood as all the departing Boomers hit the road at the stroke of midnight plus one minute.

This year, in recognition of our diminishing stamina, we're celebrating New Years' Eve at 10:00 p.m. How sad is that? But, the fact remains, we can't party like we used to. Boomer burnout is just plain humiliating so we're going to try and make it 'til the midnight hour at a friend's place after dinner. Even though *"Can't Get No Satisfaction"* may rev us up for three point five minutes, that's about all we can handle. *"When I'm sixty-four"* ceased long ago to be a look into the future and is quickly becoming the good old days for most of us. Not to be discouraged, we're still out there trying. We love shakin' it down and boogying to the fifties and sixties music as long as our hip and knee replacements hold up. Listening to Tommy James and the Shondelles or Simon and Garfunkle, I'm transported back to 1967 – the summer of love. Closing my eyes, I'm twenty again as I re-live that incredible time in our lives. Now that we're *in* our sixties, it's still great but in a different way.

When Wilson Picket sang, *"Wait 'til the midnight hour, when there's no one else around . . ."*, little did he know how prophetic it would be. Sweet dreams. 2015 is going to be a magnificent year.

Remembering Christmas past and present

A recent media piece asked people to recall their most memorable Christmas gift ever. Was it an Xbox? A new bike? Perhaps a trip to Disney World? I can honestly say that not one gift stands out as being particularly memorable for me growing up in the fifties and sixties. Christmas past for me was not about the gifts, which relative to our time were special, but it was about the experience – the events, the smells of real Christmas trees in everyone's home, the sounds and the tastes. It meant getting together with grandparents, uncles, aunts, cousins and friends who all lived in the same small Ontario town within ten minutes of each other.

Christmas day was about opening our presents and then spending the day with a house full of relatives for Christmas dinner – always the same menu – overcooked turkey, mashed potatoes and gravy (on the potatoes, not the meat), mashed turnip, peas and carrots, stuffing, canned fruit cocktail in red jello, cabbage salad, rolls and butter and a little juice glass of Heinz tomato juice. This feast was followed by homemade mincemeat pies and pumpkin pie with fresh whipped cream, homemade Christmas cake and cookies.

As Boomers, we received wonderful gifts like soft new flannelette pyjamas with snowflakes on them and perhaps a new colouring book with a fresh box of crayons. I still get a high when I open a fresh new box of Crayola's and smell all the wonderful colours.

Every year we looked forward to attending the Christmas party at the Masonic Temple put on by the mill where my Dad worked, or the Legion where, as a veteran he was President at the time. We rehearsed and put on Christmas concerts for our parents at the church. Santa was always the finale of the event and gave each one of us a little cellophane bag of hard Christmas candies and gum drops with a couple of chocolates thrown in as a special treat. We wore our very best clothes and sang "Here comes Santa Claus," "Rudolph The Red Nosed Reindeer" and "Jingle Bells."

Christmas present is rather different from what we've experienced in the past. We've evolved through the years of buying gifts for everyone on the planet, stressing over what to give to whom, entertaining 'til we dropped and getting depressed in January when life returned to normal and our Visa bill came in. My Boomer Broad friends and I are now at a nice point in life where Christmas is becoming more about the experience again. Gift-giving has gone so far over the top that we've stopped giving each other "stuff" altogether. With some of us now moving into condos, we're trying to lighten our load and get rid of material encumbrances. My friend Gail reduced her seven storage bins of

Christmas decorations to just one when she moved into a condo and none of us go to the extremes we used to. In these times of affluence we already have more than enough.

The grandchildren are mostly teenagers now and love nothing more than a cheque under the tree. I'm no longer prowling the overcrowded, overheated malls in December, grouchy as a bear, searching for that elusive gift for whomever. No gifts = no stress = a very merry Christmas indeed.

The best part about Christmas present is a return to the joy of Christmas past. Once again, it's all about the experience of setting the big long table with Christmas dishes, surrounding that table with loved ones, whether friends, family or both, and savouring the sounds, smells, tastes and hugs that go with the season. Think I'll go watch The Christmas Story where Ralphie shoots his eye out with his new BB gun – a little slice of Christmas past to enjoy in the present. And to you, a good night.

Breaker, breaker. Do 'ya read me good buddy?

Have we really come a long way baby? About forty years ago, in the olden days before cell phones, we had the CB (Citizens' Band) radio. Remember them? My first husband was a bit of a zealot and installed one in our car and our boat so he could keep in touch with his guy friends while on the move. Popular with truckers, CBs were the communication link that allowed them to inform their good-buddies of their exact "twenty" (location) and other seemingly vital daily minutia.

CB users had their own idiom with secret codes and abbreviations for various common expressions. Chatting to each other when driving to the cottage or boat, CB'ers would warn of "Smokies" (police) so the following car could avoid radar or at least slow down. Many of them set these radios up in their homes to listen to and chat with others at any hour. I thought it was embarrassingly juvenile, like little boys playing with walkie-talkies. This, despite the fact a hugely successful movie, Smokey & The Bandit starring Burt Reynolds and Jackie Gleason also starred a CB radio in a leading role used to facilitate the smuggling of beer.

Fast-forward to 2014 and technology looks quite different today. It's advancing and changing so rapidly I can hardly keep up. We now have texts, blips, tweets and apps for our cell phones that make James Bond's gadgets look prehistoric. Cell phones and e-mail in their various forms have become the twenty-first century's CB radio. It's the new millennium's way of enabling our basic need to keep in touch, to communicate with other human beings, albeit through an inhuman medium. Even the most benign daily events are now text-worthy, so much so that some people even risk their lives and mine to do it while driving.

Has the keyboard replaced human contact? Can an LOL really replace a good belly laugh when sharing a joke with your BFF over a pot of tea? Eye contact is becoming as scarce as Phillip Lim purses at Target. Walk into any coffee shop and witness dozens of lone customers staring at their smart phones and laptops with fingers and thumbs a blur of singular activity. Simply walking down the street has become hazardous as you dodge preoccupied texters and e-mailers looking down while walking into traffic, utility poles and even other texters. Let's hope we don't forget the importance of a real live warm hug or the sound of a room full of laughter when someone shares a story.

One of the first things I do when I get up in the morning is check my e-mail and throughout the day I constantly re-check to see if any of my inner circle (which is now widening) has a message for me. It's also one of the last things I do at night before going to bed. Don't want to take a chance on missing out on the latest news on who's e-mailing who or what they had for lunch.

The bottom line is I am now no better than my ex. Please don't tell him. It's simply too embarrassing. My blog is proof of my guilt and I tell everyone I know that if they want to know what's going on in my life, tune in. We've come full circle – but in a different band width.

BTW, my "handle" is ***boomerbroadcast.net***. 10-7 (signing off) for now. TTYL.

We had hope

With the fiftieth anniversary of the death of President Kennedy, I can hear all the Gen X'ers, Y'ers and Millenials moaning, "We don't *care* that you can remember what you were doing when you heard that Kennedy had been shot."

Well, it changed our lives forever which is a fairly significant event. What if he'd lived? Think of the possibilities. Our lives might be quite different today. He was just getting started on a seismic shift in societal attitudes that only *began* with civil rights.

Our response? We don't care that you don't care. *We* care. Back then we had hope – which is a far cry from the sad state of affairs our politicians are offering today.

P.S. Ironically, I was in grade eleven history class when the Principal knocked on the door to announce to our teacher what had happened. **Where were you, fellow Boomers?**

Oooh boy – back in my day

The differences in parenting styles between how we Boomers were raised back in the olden days and the approaches by today's young parents always makes for lively conversation. I can't believe we're actually saying things like, "Back when we were young," but it truly is so very, very different from today. I won't detail all those differences here as most of us are now grandparents and first-hand witnesses to the contrasts.

Surely we were as precocious and entertaining as kids today are. We must have said cute things, dazzled our parents with our intelligence and impressed everyone with our accomplishments. But I don't seem to remember any kind of recognition or acknowledgement of these behaviours. While our parents surely noticed, we were not encouraged to promote ourselves. That would be showing off and that was just not an acceptable behaviour. Self-esteem and recognition were simply not part of the child-rearing vocabulary in the fifties and sixties.

I was reminded of this while reading David Sedaris' latest book, *Let's Explore Diabetes With Owls*. He wrote the following paragraphs in response to seeing a young boy outside a store defacing a federal mail box with marker pens. A by-stander held the boy until the parents came out of the store and instead of disciplining him for his bad behaviour, the parents verbally attacked the bystander for touching their child. Sedaris was understandably appalled and described his own experience growing up in a family of six kids:

"I don't know how these couples do it, spend hours each night tucking their kids in, reading them books about misguided kittens or seals who wear uniforms, then rereading them if the child so orders. In my house, our parents put us to bed with two simple words: "Shut up." That was always the last thing we heard before our lights were turned off. Our artwork did not hang on the refrigerator or anywhere near it, because our parents recognized it for what it was: crap. They did not live in a child's house, we lived in theirs.

Neither were we allowed to choose what we ate. I have a friend whose seven-year-old will only consider something if it's white. Had I tried that, my parents would have said, "You're on," and served me a bowl of paste, followed by joint compound. They weren't considered strict by any means. They weren't abusive. The rules were just different back then, especially in regard to corporal punishment. Not only could you hit your own children, but you could also hit other people's."

While hitting children is obviously wrong, we still must ask, are our expectations of kids today wrong? Our generation hasn't been a total screw-up. There's a lot of talk about what will become of the generation being raised in this age of entitlement where no one ever loses, no one is second-best, and everyone thinks they can become Prime Minister or President. Dealing with failure and disappointment are part of growing up and learning to cope with life. The sun does not rise and set on each of us alone. We're part of a complex society that is not always fair or easy and the sooner we learn to cope with this fact of life the stronger we'll be. Our parents did some things right. And for that we are very thankful.

The age of entitlement

Call me insensitive but I wholeheartedly agree with Margaret Wente's recent column in The Globe and Mail, "Student debt crisis? No, crisis in expectations." I keep hearing how it's different for young people today. They have huge student debts to pay off and no hope of getting a salary to take care of it, etc. etc.

Let's step back a bit and compare Apples (today's youth) and Oranges (baby boomers). I'm an Orange – a beta baby boomer, born in 1947. Living at home was not an option when I finished high school. There were no jobs in our small Ontario town. Apart from Ryerson or university, none of the community colleges even existed when I graduated high school and left home at seventeen. So, like my graduating contemporaries I came to the city to seek my fortune in the working world.

That fortune began on July 5, 1965 with a low-level clerk-typist job at The Bell Telephone Company of Canada, as it was called then. I applied to various companies before I finished school and attended an interview with Bell at their recruiting centre at 50 Eglinton Avenue East in Toronto which ultimately resulted in a job. Recognizing me as a naive hayseed new to Toronto, the nice hiring lady at Bell referred me to a girls' residence on Gerrard Street at Yonge known as Willard Hall. It was a three-storey boarding house for young girls run by the Women's Christian Temperance Union – yes – temperance – no smoking, no alcohol and no you-know-what. Drugs were unheard of and consumed only by the low-lifes a couple of streets over on Jarvis Street. Weed was just beginning to emerge for common consumption but at that time was still a distant apparition for us Willard Hall girls.

My parents dropped me off on the front steps of Willard Hall late on a Sunday afternoon the week after school ended, with one suitcase and no money other than what I had earned and saved at various part-time jobs during high school. I was to start work on University Avenue the next day and saved money by walking to work.

I can still remember my first meal alone at Fran's restaurant on Yonge Street that Sunday – an egg salad sandwich and a glass of milk. Then I walked back up the street to begin my new adult life.

Willard Hall was a life with no TV and only two phones on each floor for about one hundred "young ladies" to share – incoming calls only. Accommodations were spartan with no showers, just old-fashioned claw-foot bathtubs for bathing. It was similar to living at the YWCA and I did it for two years, sharing a room and closet with a girl from Brighton, Ontario who worked at Eaton's.

How does that compare with the Apples of today who have full parental funding perhaps supplemented with a student loan, a portion or all of university tuition taken care of and a guarantee of financial and emotional support for the next four years? Today's Apples start university life with a car-load of stylish clothing, computers, cell phones, flat-screen TVs, fridges, sports equipment and every technical device known to human-kind, not to mention a credit card or two funded by parents.

My brother attended five years at University of Toronto on his own nickel. This was accomplished with money he saved from several part-time jobs during high school and while attending university. He needed some student loans to fill the gap but paid them back as quickly as possible. No parental support. No car. No high-priced luxuries. No fat. Period. I also took university and college courses at my own expense over the years to enhance my résumé.

My Boomer friend's son, Mark who is part of the Apple generation X frittered away his first few years after high school. By the time he decided he wanted a university education, his family was not only unable but unwilling to pay for it. Hoping for a future in technology the prospects were slim to nil without the piece of paper. To his credit, he investigated acquiring the knowledge on his own and paying for and writing the necessary exams to achieve the credits and he did it.

In the days before credit cards, we Oranges paid cash for everything, including visits to the doctor and the dentist. Today's Apples are completely "covered". What we didn't have the cash for we did not buy.

Until I got married at the age of twenty-seven, I lived in a variety of accommodations, none of them luxurious. I shared a one-bedroom apartment on Vaughan Road with two sisters who crammed two single beds into the tiny bedroom while I slept on the second-hand couch in the even-smaller living room. I once lived on the top attic floor of a cheap boarding house in Parkdale with a hot plate in the hallway and a taxi-driver in the room across the hall. The summer heat in that little attic room was unbearable. The first apartment I rented on my own was an ancient bachelor unit, again on Vaughan Road with no kitchen counters, an old claw-foot tub and an endless supply of mice. Would Gen X Apples settle for such accommodations – or more appropriately would their adoring parents let them.

Some of the jobs that I and my Orange friends have held over the years have been equally uninspiring, working for Ma Bell, insurance companies and banks. But we did them to pay the rent and buy our Kraft dinner. Moving back home was not an option. And that brings me to the crux of my argument. We Oranges did what we had to do because we had no options – there were no boomerang kids then. Parents expected us to suck it up and figure things out. After all, they had come through the Depression and had no sympathy for whiners.

As I've said before, I think the key to success in life is being "hungry" at some point along the way with no safety net. You get pretty resourceful when there's no one there to bail you out. It's character building. And, that's how one Boomer Broad from The Age of Aquarius views The Age of Entitlement. For better or worse.

Another look at the entitlement debate

One of my favourite times of the day is enjoying my second cup of tea while reading *The Globe & Mail's* essay on the Facts & Arguments page. And this morning's "Nice work – if we can get it" by Braeden Banks did not disappoint.

His honest, intelligent commentary on the reality of young graduates finding a job in today's economy was a realistic response. Braeden is obviously not one of those people seeking the perfect job in the perfect World of Oz. I applaud his resourcefulness, his determination and his lack of ego.

Braeden did all the right things, getting a university degree and college diploma. When he was unsuccessful blitzing the careers pages of every on-line company, non-profit and government institution, he followed his parents' advice to "hit the bricks", peddling his wares on foot. When his aunt and uncle told him "It's all about who you know," he texted and e-mailed everyone he'd ever met who collects a pay cheque. Ultimately he did get a job – not a career – but it's a start.

We Boomers must bear some responsibility for the difficulties encountered by the Braeden's of our world. As employers we are reluctant to hire inexperienced young graduates. Unions protect senior employees who may have passed their "best before" date. We cling to our own jobs longer than we probably should to fatten our retirement income because we did not manage our money all that well during our working years. We are often quick to judge all young people as spoiled egocentrics who do not share our work ethic.

While I now have the time to spend my weekday mornings drinking tea and blogging about whatever is on my mind, there are young people desperately needing employment. Some are worth hiring and training while others are not. You be the judge. After all, we need them to pay for our comfortable retirement. That's the Canadian way.

Memories of a teenage carhop

"Help me Rhonda, help help me Rhonda . . ."

Songs have a special way of transporting us back to the time and place when they were part of our everyday lives. Hear a certain song, close your eyes and you're drifting along in a time and place many years ago. You remember what you were doing and where you were. Maybe you were babysitting, parked with your favourite guy or just lying in your room late at night listening to WKBW in Buffalo on your transistor radio – that's the only time you could get a signal. Ahh – the mellow harmonies of the Beach Boys, *"In my room, in my room. . ."*

I never get tired of sixties music. It transports me back to weekends working at a drive-in restaurant. Not many people today can include "carhop" on their resume. From age fourteen to seventeen, I worked weekends as a carhop at a tiny little drive-in burger restaurant in our small Ontario town. The drive-in was located on a side street behind the bowling alley and just like in the movie American Graffiti everyone gathered there after doing whatever they do on a Friday or Saturday night.

We did not roller skate to our customers' cars however as the road in front of the restaurant was partially gravel but we looked pretty darned cute in white pedal pushers and sailor blouses in the summer. As fall set in, our outfits were replaced by heavy coats and gloves until about mid-November when all the action moved inside.

When cars arrived, they angle-parked in front of the drive-in or across the street and left their headlights on to indicate they wanted service. After we'd delivered the order to the car on a heavy aluminum tray that clamped to the open window on the driver's side, they'd turn their lights off. When they were ready to leave the headlights came on again to signal us to come and collect the tray and garbage. That system wouldn't work today with car headlights running as soon as you turn on the ignition.

The restaurant was probably the size of your average two-car garage. Inside were two tables for four people and a counter with eight stools – hardly a mega enterprise. On the weekends there were usually four or five of us working behind the counter flipping burgers, mixing shakes and frying fries. I can still remember the shorthand we used on the order sheets to speed things up.

CMS = chocolate milk shake

VMS, SMS, BMS for vanilla, strawberry or butterscotch

FF = French fries, or "chips" as we called them

HB = hamburger, **CB** = cheeseburger, **XO** = no onion – after all there was probably some serious making-out on the agenda for customers after they left

Order forms hung in a row on one-inch finishing nails hammered into a shelf above the grill. In the galley behind were three adjoining stainless steel sinks and when there was a lull in traffic we washed and dried all the dishes by hand. No electric dishwashers back then. Pruny hands were a way of life.

The prices were easy to remember and add up.

Milkshakes, twenty-five cents

Hamburgers, twenty-five cents

Cheeseburgers, thirty cents

Chips, fifteen cents

Ice cream cones – ten cents for one scoop, fifteen cents for two scoops

Cigarettes were thirty-five cents a pack and coffee was ten cents a cup. And you really had to put your weight behind slamming down those large round keys on the old manual cash register. Ka-ching.

Working conditions were laughable by today's standards. When I first started I was paid sixty-five cents an hour which was raised to seventy-five cents during my last year. Tips were practically non-existent as most of the customers were kids like us. On Friday and Saturday nights I worked from 6:00 p.m. to 1:00 a.m. and from noon to 6:00 p.m. on Sundays. After we closed at 1:00 a.m. the staff would sit down for a burger and shake which the owners were kind enough to sell us at half price. Then we mopped the floors, washed and dried the dishes, cleaned the single unisex washroom, cleaned the grill and generally left everything shipshape for the next day's business. And we didn't get paid for the hour between 1:00 a.m. and 2:00 a.m. when we did all the cleanup and closing up work. Then, the owners would drive us home. If they weren't there, Eddie, who also worked there, would walk us home, and then walk across town himself to go home.

Some nights we'd tune in to CKPT AM radio in Peterborough on a tiny transistor radio we'd place on the window sill of the take-out window. CHUM in Toronto was totally out of range but sometimes we'd catch a cool tune from Peterborough or Belleville when traffic was slow.

Things got really crazy during the last couple of hours before closing. The local single-screen movie theatre let out around 11:30 and the dance hall closed at midnight and by the time everyone worked their way over to the drive-in, the parking lot was jammed. Cars that weren't actually parked to buy food were cruising back and forth, back and forth with all the windows down and Beach Boys, Elvis or Tommy James and the Shondelles blaring from the radio. Ronnie Hawkins was always popular because he was almost a "local". He owned a farm near Peterborough and often played local venues. And because we were a semi-rural community, Johnny Cash, Ray Price and Conway Twitty were always popular. Friday and Saturday night cruising was the social highlight of the week after farm chores were done and school work put aside.

The really cool guys drove with their left shoulder pushed forward against the driver's door and their right arm around their chick-de-jour who would be snuggled up close on the wide bench seat. It looked like two people were driving. . . .

Sweet little Sheila, you'd know her if you see her . . .*C'mon baby, do the Loco-motion* . . .or how about *Be my little run run run run runaway* . . .

Ah, those were the days, my friend.

Those too were the days my friend

When I strolled around the CNE (Canadian National Exhibition) in Toronto on the last day on Labour Day weekend, I couldn't help reminiscing about the time I worked there as a sweet young Boomer-broad in the summer of 1968. I was working for Bell Canada at the time and in those days (before everyone was jaded by Canada's Wonderland) the annual Ex was a big deal. Kids saved their Telly fun cheques to offset the cost of the rides and everyone wanted to climb the Shell Tower to get a good overview of all the excitement. The buildings offered delights and experiences not available in today's tired old lady on the lake, including a visit to see Elsie the cow, a life-size replica of a cow carved in real butter in the food building. That display was sponsored by The Milk Marketing Board.

Large corporations staged sophisticated exhibits to showcase their wares and tantalize us with what we could look forward to in the future. I was one of more than two dozen "Bell girls" selected from within the company to be part of that year's Bell exhibit. It was housed in the Queen Elizabeth Building and consisted of two side-by-side "shows". My group of girls took turns go-go dancing in a glass tube to The Age of Aquarius by Sly and The Family Stone. We wore snazzy yellow and white crimpolene pants and tunic outfits that made us sweat like pigs. When a group of people had assembled around the dancing girl in the booth (me or one of the other Bell girls), we would pick up a new Contempra phone, the latest high-tech phone of its time which acted as a microphone and delivered our little spiel. "Hello, welcome to Bell Canada . ." followed by a five-minute memorized monologue about all the new and wonderful things Bell was working on. We demonstrated a prototype of the futuristic "Picture-phone" which included a snowy black and white television screen showing a live view of whoever you were talking to. That demonstration was met with a great deal of 1968 skepticism about "what if you're in your pyjamas and you don't want anyone to see you." Little did we know what the future would bring in terms of iPhones, Skype and the other high-tech snooping devices we now use daily.

The other half of our Bell exhibit was a magic show by part of our contingent on an adjoining stage with seating for an audience of about 100 people. We worked in shifts and kept CNE visitors entertained and informed for the duration of the "EX". It was especially enjoyable for me because, not only was it an honour to be selected but I lived in a tiny apartment on Spencer Avenue near the exhibition grounds so I could walk to work, saving the cost of transit tokens. And I got to eat EX junk food for my meal break every day. I clearly remember the wonderful smell of frying onions as I walked along the midway to my lunch-spot-de-jour. Bell offered to sell us our outfits at cost after the EX closed but after two weeks of sweating in it and washing and wearing it every day, I'd had enough. Still, it was an experience I treasure and will never forget.

In Praise of Cursive Writing

Just when I'm thinking I should brush up on my cursive handwriting skills I hear that many schools aren't even teaching it anymore. The downside of that brilliant move is that many young people cannot read written documents unless the words appear as type on a tablet, computer, smart phone or printed document.

As a left-handed writer in grade two (in the fifties) I was one of the last kids in the class to advance from a fat "learner's" pencil to the sleek yellow HP when it was time to begin learning cursive. Later, we all had to learn to write with ink using a fountain pen and each of us had a little bottle of ink in the round hole on our wooden desks for refilling our pens. Writing with a fountain pen when you're left-handed presents a number of challenges. We were disciplined to hold our pens a certain way—index finger on the top of the barrel with thumb parallel on the bottom with the writing instrument resting on the knuckle of the second finger. And your arm was to be parallel to the *side* of the page.

This regimen meant lefties dragged their hand over the wet ink, smearing their writing. The solution was to crook your arm ninety degrees so it was parallel to the *top* of the page (like Barack Obama and Prince William) which looked odd and resulted in teachers slamming your knuckles with a ruler until you did it properly. At least that was better than in my father's day when lefties were forced to write with their right hand.

As a left-handed writer, it's always been difficult for me to execute the kind of gentle, sweeping curves I would like to achieve. This is the result of lefties having to "push" the pen across the page as opposed to the "drawing" across the page by righties. This may be difficult for right-handed writers to understand but Leonardo Da Vinci understood. Leonardo was left-handed and found it infinitely easier to write backwards with his quill and ink—that is, right to left on the page rather than left to right. This mirror-writing is relatively easy for lefties to execute because we get to "draw" the pen across the page, a more fluid operation than pushing. I remember writing to a pen-pal when I was in high school entirely in mirror-writing so she had to hold it up to a mirror to read it. I get 'ya Leonardo.

The look of beautiful cursive handwriting always fascinates me and I've only seen two people in recent years whose writing qualifies. There's nothing quite as lovely as reading a note, a letter or a card written in liquid washable blue ink with an old-fashioned fountain pen. Ballpoints just don't have the same cachet. As a result of using computer keyboards for most of my writing these days, my never-that-great handwriting is starting to resemble the scratchings of a demented illiterate. It's the old, "if you don't use it, you lose it".

For many years I've searched for the perfect pen for handwritten notes. Most fountain pens are too scratchy and are not leftie-friendly. Recently, after trying a number of different brands of gel and roller pens I purchased a nice little number at Staples by Pentel called EnerGel, Liquid Gel Ink plunger-style pen. And I love it. The washable blue colour and smooth delivery of the ink is as close as I can get to the fountain-pen look I like. Now all I have to do is get a lined exercise book and start practising my upper and lowercase letters until they resemble the artistic cursive I would like to see. If no one comes along and cracks my knuckles with a ruler, I might just get better. Mrs. Thompson would be proud. Maybe I could even be trusted to use a grown-up pen.

Seventeen soldiers are moving in on Monday

What would your reaction be if a military officer showed up at your front door and told you he was going to billet a dozen soldiers in your home for an indeterminate length of time and you had to provide meals and laundry service for them? And you had no choice in the matter. I was reminded of this prospect as I was watching *Mr. Selfridge* on PBS' Masterpiece Theatre on Sunday night about the founder of the famous Selfridge's department store on Oxford Street in London, England. In this week's episode, World War I has started and one of the store employees has a Belgian refugee billeted in her home.

    This actually happened to my grandmother's family in 1914 in Folkestone, England (on the White Cliffs of Dover). My great-grandmother was a widow with sons who had enlisted for service and she was left at home with three daughters, the eldest being my grandmother who was in her early twenties at the time. As a result of thousands of young men enlisting to train and fight in The Great War (WWI), there was a shortage of barracks. One day an army officer knocked on the door of their terraced house and asked how many soldiers my grandmother's family could accommodate. Her reply, "Probably three".

    My grandmother then described how "the Major asked to go through the house and informed my mother that we would be taking **seventeen soldiers** into our home" and they would be receiving a stipend for housing them and giving them their meals every day.

    Later on in the war as the various allotments of soldiers were rotated out, their house was requisitioned to provide accommodation for Belgian refugees —women and children. My grandmother had many amazing stories about these experiences. She and her sisters enjoyed the social life which included going to dances with all the soldiers. She described how some of the soldiers billeted in their home were illiterate miners from the north of England who had never been exposed to such things as how to use table cutlery and basic hygiene such as bathing and brushing your teeth. One hundred years later, this kind of scenario seems unimaginable. But it was a widespread practice during the war and every family "did their bit".

    I always loved my grandmother's stories and now that she's gone and I'm older, I can think of so many questions I wish I'd asked her. She was engaged twice previously—once to an Englishman and once to another Canadian, before marrying my Canadian grandfather on Armistice Day, November 11, 1918. Both of her previous fiancés and a brother had been killed in France. She recounted how, when they walked out of the photographer's studio after their wedding, all the church bells were ringing and people were dancing in the streets. She thought everyone was celebrating her wedding but in fact, the Armistice had been signed while they were in the photographer's. In 1919 she left England behind and boarded a ship bound for Halifax with hundreds of British war brides sailing to join their new husbands in Canada.

Watching the news on TV today about the horror of nearly two hundred schoolgirls being kidnapped in Nigeria, the ongoing wars in the Middle East and the living conditions of other innocent citizens in regions of conflict, we need to always be thankful for being born in Canada. Hopefully an army officer will never knock on our doors and tell us we have seventeen soldiers moving in. And for that we can be eternally grateful.

Chapter 2
People

*All You Need is Love
. . . The Beatles, 1967*

Grand Parenting Boomer-style

Hillary Clinton has been the target of much undeserved speculation about her ability and commitment to her future role as candidate for President of the United States. The reason? She's going to be a grandmother later this year. Was this an issue for Bush Sr., Ronald Reagan or any other President for that matter? Mitt Romney has an entire battalion of grandchildren but no one mentioned that as a liability. In fact, male politicians often use their children and grandchildren as promotional props in their campaigns.

Being a grandparent today is different from when we Boomers were growing up. Our grandparents (if they were still alive) were grey-haired, kindly souls we visited on Sundays and could always be counted on for treats. Grandmothers were great cooks who baked pies, had old-fashioned furniture in their homes, perhaps treated themselves to a "wash and set" once a week and wore flowered dresses. They taught us to knit and bake cookies. Today's grandmothers attend yoga retreats, have a large circle of crazy-busy friends, get regular mani-pedi's, vacation in Italy, run their own businesses, drink a lot of wine and listen to Bob Dylan on their ear buds.

With Mother's Day approaching, we should take time appreciate the role our mothers and grandmothers played in fashioning the wonderful women we are today. Our lives and lifestyles are very different from what they experienced and our grandchildren will redefine it again. My own grandmother was an enormous influence on my life. As a war bride from England in the First World War, she was strong, broadminded and spirited. Her stories were the catalyst for my looking at a life outside the small Ontario town I grew up in.

As Beta Boomer Broads (BBBs – killer Bs), our generation can't be counted on to bake pies and act "grandmotherly" in the traditional sense. But our grandchildren can count on us to have strong political opinions, be somewhat technically savvy, be physically fit, eat healthy food and dress like we care how we look. We're probably going to be too busy running half-marathons and flying off for a girls' week to be there for soccer practices. The thing is, most of our grandchildren are now being raised in cities and even countries hundreds and thousands of miles away, where their parents moved for better jobs. We're not that accessible in so many ways.

None of my eight step-grandchildren live close by and their lives are also extremely busy with school, activities, friends and life in general. They all have wonderful parents who are doing an amazing job, which is a credit to their own mother and father. Before long, they'll be grandparents too and it will be interesting to see how that generation evolves. I'm pretty sure baking pies will soon become a lost art completely. It's getting harder to tell parents from grandparents when you see people with children in the mall. Parents are now having their children at ages when previous generations were grandparents. It just gets more and more interesting. As time goes on, everyone will continue to adapt to our changing social environment. Fortunately for our grandchildren, they'll hopefully have had the benefit of hearing Bob Dylan played at Grandma's house. Yes. The times, they are a' changing.

Girlfriends, the staff of life

"To love honour and cherish," are words that have been uttered with much conviction in front of family and friends by most of us in our lifetime. They convey to our spouses what we naively believe to be true until death do us part. Sadly, more than fifty percent of us, however, never fulfill those promises. In fact, it has been my experience that these words more appropriately apply to those individuals who often turn out to be the most important people in our adult lives – our girlfriends. The fact that our relationships with girlfriends are so intense, honest and enduring, without blowing a year's salary on a fancy wedding speaks volumes about the power and strength of friendships.

My own strong relationships with girlfriends began in high school and were the direct result of being totally unappealing to the opposite sex. Despite numerous crushes on classmates and other cute guys in town who cruised into the drive-in burger joint where I worked on weekends, no one was particularly interested in dating a skinny, pimply, toothy me. Undaunted, though, I bravely attended all the high school dances and did the twist, the mashed potato and jive with my girlfriends. We sat out the slow dances. I did once summon up the nerve to ask a cute blond guy called Chuck to a Sadie Hawkins dance at our high school. Having no experience with talking to boys, I asked a similarly afflicted girlfriend what we should talk about. She wisely advised, "talk about his interests". (Some things never change, do they?) I knew he belonged to the wrestling club so I cleverly started a conversation with, "So I hear you belong to the wrestling club?" to which he replied, "Yes.". End of conversation. Beginning of a very long painful evening. His mother probably made him honour the date with me because it was the kind thing to do.

Fifty years later, it's still girlfriends I can always count on to advise, support, humour and honour me when I need it. The day I separated from my first husband, I landed on my girlfriend's doorstep in tears at 9:30 in the morning. She immediately put the kettle on, dropped whatever she had planned for that day and listened, sympathized and supported my soul for the entire day while I blubbered. Comedienne Sandra Shamas in one of her shows described her own marital separation something like this, "When a woman is in pain, she emits a strong, silent signal that is audible only to other women. And then they come. Friends descend with love, caring and boxes of cookies and squares and pots of tea." It's a very powerful energy.

Friends share secrets, diet tips, fashion advice, books and even other friends. We share and support each other through the process of aging, bolstered by the thought that we're not alone. The other day as I removed a small packet of hearing aid batteries from my purse, we had a good laugh recalling that it doesn't seem that long ago we were retrieving tampons from similar packets in our purses. Sharing hangover remedies has been replaced by fibre recommendations. Listening to confessions about love life disasters has happily been overtaken by loving life. Getting rid of unwanted hair has been superseded by efforts to conquer hair loss. We're all in this together.

My network of girlfriends is large. Some I've known since kindergarten, more than sixty years ago. Others are more recent but most of my circle of friends has been around for at least forty years. They're smart, funny, kind and generous. We've seen each other through the good, the bad and the ugly. Husbands have come and gone. Children have grown up and left home which freed us up for more time together. We've watched one another lose our waistlines and gain some wrinkles. Some have lost husbands, children, parents and other friends. But we still have each other. For better, for worse, for richer, for poorer, 'til death do us part.

Husbands are not girlfriends

In the February 2014 issue of Oprah Magazine, author Anna Quindlen offers up the following quote as one of the "Five Things I Know for Sure":

"I can't get by without my friends. I often hear brides say their groom is their best friend. Really? My husband is my husband. My best friend is someone who has the patience to listen to a monologue about the heinously expensive purse I want. When I'm falling, my girlfriends are my soft landing."

Amen, Anna!

Father's Day and the family tree

My eighty-eight year old Dad just planted a new variety of apple tree in his back yard because he "likes to watch them grow and bear fruit". He already has several fruit trees and enjoys nurturing them through the various seasons. He's had some success with grafting and at one point had four varieties of apples on a single tree. Obviously he doesn't put much stock in the old adage about not buying green bananas. After all, my parents only go grocery shopping once a week so bananas *have* to be green to last.

Still living in and managing your own home and garden at eighty-eight is commendable. Dad still cuts his own grass and with the help of a snow blower he clears his own driveway in the winter. When the snow on the roof was reaching unsafe levels this past winter, he carved a path to the front window so he could reach part of the roof with the snow rake to pull the weight off the roof. He also cleared a path in the deep snow to the end of his garden so he could cart out their daily organic waste to the compost bin. My parents eat fresh vegetables from their garden all summer and into the fall and winter. And now he has a new apple tree to tend to.

I hope my Dad's optimism and love of such simple things as a tree is still with me when I'm eighty-eight. We planted a rather sad little weeping Cyprus tree at our house and as I watch it grow into a beautiful tree in the years to come, I'll be reminded of my father and his optimistic little apple tree.

Father's Day is a chance for those of us who still have our fathers to be thankful for what we have and for those who have lost their fathers, to be thankful for what they had. After all, they're the roots of our family tree.

Don't never talk to strangers

Yes. It's a double negative. Now that I'm retired and not rushing head-down in a panic all the time, I have more time to observe life and in particular, to people-watch. This new preoccupation has led to an increase in my engaging strangers in quick conversation which usually takes the form of a comment as I'm passing by. Food courts seem to be particularly conducive to making new friends. Yesterday as I was enjoying my fast-food lunch at Sherway Gardens in Toronto, I kept watching the young woman sitting at the next table eating lunch with her boyfriend (they were sharing food so I assumed they also share other things.). She was pretty in a plain, quiet way and had the most beautiful large gray-green eyes. As I picked up my tray to leave, I leaned over to her and said, "I'm sure you've been told this before, but you have the most drop-dead gorgeous eyes". She lit up like a Christmas tree and I felt like I'd made her day. The lovely part is that it helped make my day too.

My habit of engaging strangers in a one-sided conversation began with babies. I can never resist peeking into a stroller and complimenting the mother on how beautiful her precious little one is. I particularly love natural red hair and cannot pass an adult or child in the mall or on the street without leaning in and commenting positively on their red hair as I pass by.

The other day I was in a kitchen store being served by a beautiful, somewhat shy young sales clerk. I began our conversation by telling her how pretty she was and what beautiful skin she had. She immediately relaxed and we then engaged in a lovely conversation about the store products. Passing along compliments to strangers is a free way of "paying it forward" when they don't come with an ulterior motive. Retail sales personnel are the most transparent opportunists for finding at least one thing about your appearance to compliment when you enter their store. They've been trained to know it makes you feel better and you're more likely to spend money in their store.

Again in a food court the other day I sat next to a couple of high school girls, one of whom was wearing a tee shirt with the Beatles' Revolver album imprinted on the front. That's talking my language and I couldn't resist commenting to the girl wearing it. "I loved that album thirty years before you were even born" I said. Both girls laughed and seemed to appreciate the attention.

My motive for passing along these compliments and observations is not only because it makes the other person feel great, but I feel better too. When I tell the checkout clerk at Superstore that I love her haircut her face lights up and I'm sure she appreciates hearing a positive remark in a day that probably has had more than its share of complaints and she's been on her feet all day. Positive feedback is so uplifting.

Boomer Broads are a generation raised to downplay compliments in case we're thought to be "showing off". When someone tells us we're looking particularly snazzy, our reply often is something like, "Oh this old top. I've had it forever." Like my contemporaries, I've had to train myself to accept compliments graciously and appreciate the good intention. My habit of engaging in conversation with strangers seems to be on the increase. Which means I can look forward to opening up even more opportunities for feeling good? Spread a little sunshine.

Hey! Look up

When we Boomers were in our twenties, navel gazing was considered a waste of time. We were told to get out there and do something and we did, whether it took the form of getting an education or a job, expanding our circle of friends, backpacking around Europe or marching in protest to a variety of issues we did not agree with.

It appears to me that everyone today is not looking outward and upward but literally down and inward. Smart phones have become the overriding tool of communication and whether sitting in coffee shops, walking down the street, riding the subway and unfortunately even while driving everyone is looking down, literally. How can this not translate into inaction and inertia?

In retrospect I often wish I'd been a more involved participant in the events that characterized the lives of Boomers in the 1960's and 70's. I only protested once and that was in the 1980's when I set up a card table at a Queen's Park rally selling tee-shirts I'd had made up that said "Taxed to the Max and Rae-ving Mad!" when I objected to Bob Rae's style of government. I sent some tee shirts to Conrad Black who kindly sent me a personal thank you note which I kept as a souvenir for a very long time.

I lived downtown during that incredible time in the sixties and seventies. We walked everywhere rather than spend money on subway tokens, taking in events at Toronto Island, attending dances at Ryerson and parties at University of Toronto frat houses. Friday and Saturday nights were spent walking back and forth along Yorkville Avenue listening to the beat of music coming from The Riverboat, The Purple Onion and other clubs, swaying with the summer crowd and draft-dodgers (thanks U.S. for sending us those guys who ultimately were a great asset to Canada) in our psychedelic blouses and bell bottoms. CHUM AM radio (we didn't have a TV at Willard Hall where I lived) kept us up to date on the radical goings-on at Rochedale College and there was always something to do and somewhere to go. We loved standing outside The Coq D'Or on Yonge Street peeking in the open door and through the smoke listening to Ronnie Hawkins who sometimes graced us with a visit on the street. The drinking age was twenty-one then and at nineteen we weren't old enough to go in. Fake ID never even occurred to us.

There's a documentary series called *The Sixties* currently running on CNN and as I watch it each Thursday night I'm reminded of all the activity generated by Boomers at that time. The music was and still is magical. Our interest in politics was intense and we didn't hesitate to make ourselves heard. The closest thing I've seen to that kind of passion recently was the limp and ineffective "Occupy Wall Street" movement which fizzled out. The bad guys got away with it. Ho hum. Back to checking e-mails and texting what we had for lunch.

As someone who rarely uses her cellphone and doesn't even know how to text, I may sound like a complete dinosaur but it frees me up to look around and observe the world around me. It provides me with a ton of material to blog about and my laptop has become my old-lady version of marching with a protest sign. I worry that we're becoming too complacent about what the bad guys are doing to us. The recent Ontario election is a perfect example. We had a sorry choice no matter who we voted for. Do we vote for another four years of reckless fiscal management (Liberals), tuned-out slash and burn (Conservatives) or scary, myopic socialism (NDP—I still haven't forgotten the damage done by Rob Rae).

I'm probably wasting my time trying to be heard when everyone around me is preoccupied looking down at their smartphones. Now that Boomers are retiring and have time to make ourselves heard, I hope we do just that. From housing for seniors to relevant entertainment to pensions, we have to protect our interests. Pierre Trudeau's reckless debt incursion and the Vietnam War were mistakes that are still being felt to this day. Why do we keep letting the bad guys do bad things to us? I keep hoping that one by one, people will eventually look up and out from their Smartphones at what is really going on and do something to put it right. But I'm not optimistic

How lucky can one girl get?

I promised my husband I wouldn't write about him, but since he doesn't read my material anyway and I know I can count on you to keep it to yourself, this one was just too good to resist. His Christmas present to me this year was the coup de grace, home run, the grand slam of gift-for-your-wife faux pas – not one, not two but a set of *three* crock pots – one medium size and two little ones. Combined with the large five-quart Crock Pot I already own I'll be able to open a concession stand at the CNE selling hot dogs. Am I not the luckiest girl in the world? To be fair, he did consult me ahead of time – told me he saw them at Sam's Club and was very impressed. While I gently stated that I thought I could manage without them, he got more excited and it became obvious he really wanted to buy them. Guys clearly love gadgets with electrical cords no matter how useless they are. Part of his responsibility for giving me such a precious gift included finding a place to store them. After a great deal of clanging and banging, he managed to clear out the top shelf of the cupboard in the laundry room so now they're all safe and sound – and out of sight! I'm truly, truly blessed.

He also got me a nice book that I'm enjoying and in order to pre-empt complete and utter catastrophe on the gift front, I had preselected, purchased and placed under the tree, a lovely little Tiffany's blue box for Lynda containing a pendant on a silver chain. Whew! Saved by the credit card. I am indeed a very lucky girl.

Fathers know best

I just discovered that for the past three years my husband has been putting powder dishwashing detergent into the *rinse agent* receptacle of our dishwasher instead of the *detergent* receptacle. That probably explains why I have a white powdery residue on the inside of my dishwasher. I could trade him in but he cooks two nights a week so he comes with benefits.

Still swinging in her sixties

Although I subscribe to eighteen magazines each month, *Good Housekeeping* isn't one of them. But when I happened to spot the glossy lavender cover of the September 2013 British edition in Chapters, I couldn't resist. It featured a picture of one of the original Boomer babes, Twiggy looking pretty great at sixty plus-something. Eager to learn her secrets to ageless aging, I bought a copy and it was a surprisingly fun read. The pictures of her were flattering bearing in mind that Brit mags don't photo-shop their material to surreal extremes like the American ones. Still pleasingly slim, she had some interesting comments. One I liked, when asked about her personal style mantra, she replied, *"Style is about finding your look. My style has evolved over many years. I hate it when people say you have to wear certain things in your thirties, forties and fifties. It's insane! My daughter and I go shopping together. We'll sometimes buy the same jeans or jacket, but we wear it differently."* I thought that was rather clever. I now have permission to buy some biker boots and a leather moto-cross jacket. Only I have to wear them with perfectly tailored jeans and maybe some pearls or my diamond studs. Twiggy's not the only one who's cool in her sixties.

Chapter 3
Places

Hey, You, Get Off Of My Cloud,
. . . Rolling Stones, 1966

Build it and Boomers will come

As a Beta Boomer I'm at the front edge of Baby Boomers entering retirement years. We're a different kettle of sashimi from earlier generations and the type of accommodation we're looking for as we age is very specific and practically non-existent. In metropolitan areas such as Toronto and Vancouver, the land and real estate prices work against us but that's often exactly where we want to be so we're close to hospitals, doctors, entertainment, friends and family. I tried living in cottage country for several years (in two different locations) and the novelty soon wore off as I found myself trekking up and down Highway 400 several times a week to meet friends in the city or take care of my urban urges.Over the years I've made my home in pretty much every type of accommodation there is. I've lived in a girls' residence, bed-sits, bachelor apartments, condo apartments, country homes, city homes and suburban townhomes. Now that I'm retired I'm nice and comfy in a two-storey suburban home with a small, beautiful yard. However, we're reaching an age where it would be nice to have everything on one level.

As I review the retirement homes advertised in newspapers and magazines I'm consistently disappointed at the total lack of understanding of what Boomers want in retirement accommodation. Or perhaps builders do understand and simply chose to ignore us thinking they'll make us adapt to what they are offering. NOT GOING TO HAPPEN. Here's my wish list of Top Ten requirements of Baby Boomer retirement homes for the **fifteen-or-so years before we go into Assisted Living:**

1. **Single level.** No tripping on stairs as we carry laundry and groceries.
2. **Huge closets.** Boomer Broads have large wardrobes with dozens of pairs of shoes and purses. Our guys are the same, minus the purses although they do have computer bags, golf bags, gym bags and sadly, too many pairs of baggy pants. Dinky two-sliding-door closets will never

do. We want our closets to be the size of a small bedroom so we can build in shelves, racks and drawers for everything. And stop trying to stick wire shelves at the end of a clothes closet and call it a linen closet. We want a separate linen closet for towels, sheets and our overflowing cosmetics and toiletry items. And put this closet where it's logical—in the bathroom where we use most of the stuff.

3. **Kitchen pantries**. We finally have the time to indulge ourselves in cooking and baking—time we rarely had during our working years. We want out-of-sight accessible storage shelves for all our staples and small appliances. This does not mean fewer kitchen cupboards. We want both pantry space and lots of cupboards with *drawers* not shelves on the bottom.

4. **Dining area**. We don't want a separate room but an area off the kitchen or living room so we can have a few people over for dinner when the table is extended. We also like to spread the morning paper out at this table (still preferable to reading it on an iPad) so if it is next to a window that's a bonus.

5. **His & Her space**. We each have laptops and prefer our own "office" space which can be incorporated into the second bedroom, den or corner of the master bedroom or living room. His space must be able to accommodate a large flat-screen TV and La-Z-Boy.

6. **Open concept**. We've tried it and we like it. Having the kitchen and living areas open to each other is conducive to conversation and socializing.

7. **Heated bathroom floors**. This little luxury is not expensive and saves us littering the floor with scatter mats.

8. **Generous front hall closet.** See item 1 above. We have a lot of jackets, shoes and boots.

9. **Parking for two vehicles**. We're used to each having our own wheels, at least while we're still able. For one-

vehicle couples, the extra space is always good for resale and for guest parking. This parking should be underground where our vehicles are safe and dry when we go away.

10. **Accessible location.** When we want to take in the latest show at the ROM, AGO or downtown theatre we want to be able to easily access a bus, subway or GO-Train rather than fight downtown traffic.

We like granite countertops, high-end appliances (those of us who have saved our money and can afford them), wireless communication, engineered hardwood floors, crown moldings, large windows for plenty of light, outdoor areas such as small gardens, terraces or balconies so we can still grow our herbs and annuals and sit outside in nice weather. Outdoor gas hookups for barbecues on our terraces would be appreciated too.

Obviously the eight hundred and nine hundred square foot retirement homes being marketed and built now will never do. Somewhere in the neighbourhood of eighteen hundred to two thousand square feet would be lovely for couples and less for singles. Boomers are more active, more social and for better or worse more materialistic than our predecessors and we need the space to live comfortably and viably. This must also include some kind of property management to oversee maintenance issues and provide a level of home security while we travel.

In multi-unit buildings we prefer low-rise so we can get to know some of our neighbours and not have to ride into the stratosphere or waste time waiting for elevators. Community rooms are nice but we don't need gymnasiums and pools in the building. They're too expensive to maintain and add proportionately too much to monthly maintenance fees. Those people who want to use such facilities can go to local community centres at much less cost. We may be comfortable financially but we're not stupid about our money and we spend it carefully.

A boutique-type building would suit us best in terms of multi-unit accommodation. Florida is chock-a-block with well-designed condos that would do well here. I envision a six-plex or eight-plex with two condos flanking a central elevator on each floor as perfect, with windows on three sides and a south-facing terrace. Underground parking, bike storage and storage lockers are essential.

There are some wonderful retirement communities with adorable bungalows, condos and townhomes at affordable prices in small towns throughout Ontario but ***nothing in the Greater Toronto Area that is reasonably priced and meets my requirements.*** Despite years of keeping my eyes open for the kind of accommodation I would like to live in before I land in the assisted living facility, I don't see it. At the risk of sounding sexist, men do not make good residential designers as they generally do not have to make the space work—women do. Function is more important than form when laying out kitchens, bathrooms and closets and most men just don't get it.

I hope some developer who is also a Boomer with a wife who has a lot of shoes and purses will take up the challenge. We have approximately fifteen of the best years of our life between retirement and assisted living. If you build what we want, where we want, I guarantee my Boomer friends will come.

Gardiner Expressway problem solved

Who is the genius responsible for the handling of road construction work in the Toronto area? In my opinion there is absolutely no reason the Gardiner Expressway reconstruction and rehabilitation work has to take two years. For that matter, why does any road construction take so long? Have you not been tempted to scream in frustration as you sit in a traffic jam on the 401 highway across Toronto observing several lanes of traffic being funneled down to two narrow lanes—and no one is working on the bloody construction?

My corporate life was spent in commercial construction so I know a fair bit about the business. The company I worked for built more than two billion dollars in new office towers, hospitals, universities, subways and shopping centres every year. We could construct and turn over a twenty-storey office building faster than the road builders could complete a half-mile of highway. The reason for this usually came down to budget issues. It seems that governments (at whatever level) are prepared to release only so much money each year for necessary improvements and repairs to roads and highways. Therefore, it takes forever and very few resources are corralled to get the job done.

The Gardiner Expressway work could be easily accomplished by employing the P3 approach to construction. Don't believe the naysayers who deride this way of building infrastructure. P3 does not mean the private sector owns the project. Here's how it works. P3 stands for Public/Private/Partnership. Basically, it allows governments (the public component) to engage a consortium of architects, engineers, builders, financiers and managers (the private component) in a three-way partnership to build a project for which the government does not have the available money.

The private consortium contributes the necessary capital and amortizes the cost over a mutually-agreed-upon time frame, say ten years, so their costs are spread out over the agreed-to time frame and the government owns the project. Quite simply, the government has taken out a mortgage to get it built and operating as quickly as possible, while retaining ownership, with the help of the private sector's money and resources. It's a win/win scenario.

If I were running Toronto (and sometimes I think I should be, considering the mayor we have), I would put the Gardiner Expressway project out for a competitive, prequalified P3 bid to proven teams who would be tasked with getting the job done in six months at most – perhaps with a bonus for completing earlier. A private contractor could then employ three shifts working 24/7, staffing the job for maximum productivity and getting the job done. It's not that complicated. Let's put some real brains behind it.

I could live here

Last year I toured the Princess Margaret Lottery's 2013 home in Oakville. This year's model was particularly interesting because the interior was designed by Brian Gluckstein whose taste is always impeccable.

There was one major item that disappointed me, however, and it's the same every year. Why-oh-why-oh-why do they always put the laundry room in the basement? Perhaps if you have live-in help that would explain it but even with help, someone who can afford a house like that could afford another laundry room on the second floor handy to the master suite so the lady of the house doesn't have to hike miles to wash her frillies. The well-appointed laundry room included a big flat-screen TV to keep you entertained while you spool sheets and table cloths through the Miele electric mangle for professional-looking pressed linens. The laundry room is located in the northeast corner of the lower level (aka basement) while the master suite is located at the opposite end of the house in the southwest corner of the second floor. Why can't they corral a few square feet to add a laundry room on the second floor?

Otherwise, the place is truly a dream home. The kitchen and family room have huge south-facing windows for plenty of light and observing the seasons. The back yard is efficient and beautifully landscaped. And it backs onto a church parking lot so privacy is assured.

If you visit the home, be sure to wear socks. I wore sandals and had to tramp around in my bare feet with my shoes in a bag which made me uncomfortable. Understandably, they want to keep the floors and finishes clean. And while you're at it, buy a ticket or several to support the Princess Margaret Hospital. There are zillions more prizes.

It's all about being organized

As a Virgo I naturally love stores like The Container Store (www.containerstore.com) in the U.S. and Solutions (www.solutions-stores.ca) in Canada. All those endless bins and organizers appeal to my innate Virgo sense of order. I could (and have) spent hours fingering the jewellery hangers, the belt racks and OMG the kitchen wares. But a lot of my organizational tricks are practically free and work beautifully at keeping my life ticking along. Here are a couple of examples.

Before I retired, every day at the office started with a list of things to do. Stroking off each item gave me a sense of accomplishment. When I employed that system at home for household chores, I ended up with pages of messy, marked-up lists.

My solution was to write each chore on a sticky note and stick it on the kitchen cupboard door in front of my nose. Sometimes I start the day with a dozen stickies which I remove one by one as the chore is done. And I re-cycle these in a drawer. It includes such chores as ironing, laundry, walk the dog, do my nails, clean powder room, etc.

Another organizational compulsion that girlfriends tease me about is the small, round metal-framed paper hanging tags on my black pants in the closet. Most of us have multiple pairs of black pants of varying fabrics, cuts and even sizes. When I scan them by eye hanging in my closet it's hard to tell the boot-leg ones from the skinnies or the size 12s from the size 8s. In the semi-light of a closet these tags instantly tell me the pants are "dress black straight leg" or "NYDJ zips at the ankle" without having to pull each pair out and examine them individually. I'm not really neurotic, am I?

Saving Detroit

As everyone is aware, the City of Detroit is in the toilet – broke, battered and beaten. Having given it some thought, I've come up with a solution that could help everyone. Turn Detroit into Florida north. That is, make it a haven for retiring Boomers and the arts community. Homes can be purchased for next to nothing – in some cases as low as one dollar. We love fixing things up and decorating. Retirees bring all kinds of jobs and benefits that could help re-build the city. We like to eat out – restaurants would flourish, especially ones with early bird specials and happy hours. We like to wear fashionable clothes. Bring on the colorful boutiques with statement jewelry and pants with discreet adjustable waists. We also like lots of fancy shoes, although we only wear them for the above-mentioned restaurant outings.

Boomers need doctors – all kinds – ear doctors, eye doctors, plastic surgeons, hairdressers, a Walgreens on every corner and being so close to Canada, preferably a Tim Horton's on the opposite corner.

Until the safety and security issues get sorted out, we could set up gated communities where Boomers could blissfully dance to the fifties and sixties music in the Activity Centre on Friday and Saturday nights. Hell – Motown is the soul of Boomer music. We could grow our own weed and tomatoes, play tennis, golf and poker, set up book clubs and take Zumba, painting and yoga classes on weekday mornings.

Weather permitting, we could bike to visit friends or hop onto our golf carts. We'd load up on the cheap booze at Costco and Sam's Club and big screen televisions would fly off the shelves. Movie theatres would be as busy in the afternoons as the evenings as we tend to go to bed by 9:00 p.m.

We're all computer literate so there'd be plenty of jobs for young people who know how to solve our computer crashes. We no longer have the patience required and we pay big dollars to make our computer problems just go away. Mani-pedi salons would flourish. Although we like gardening we don't like cutting grass or doing heavy work. More jobs for landscapers.

Boomers all tend to drive big, expensive SUVs under the pretext they're safer although we know it's really because men still think bigger is better. The car lots and gas stations would be weeping for joy. And we're multiple-car households. Home Depot would never want for customers or hired help.

For those Boomers who still like to go to Florida (the real one down south) in winter to avoid Detroit's shitty winters, we hire house-sitters, snow shovellers, and security services to look after our northern digs while we're away. More jobs. And during the winter, the arts community could be painting our kitchens and creating more big jewelry for us to wear when we return in April. I know. I'm brilliant. Just call me.

Chapter 4
Mind

California Dreamin'
. . . The Mamas & the Papas, 1965

Have you found your passion?

Each of us is born with at least one special gift. For some it might be musical ability or for others a facility for languages. While athletes work hard to achieve greatness, they are usually equipped with special aptitudes or physical attributes conducive to their sport.

My friend Gail is skilled at crafts and artwork. Perry is a talented artist while Terry loves tennis and is really good at it. Others excel at golf. My husband is a wizard with numbers while I can't add anything with more than two digits.

All my life I've observed and envied people who have found what they love to do and do it well. I've tried many things over the years and as I enter life's third trimester I'm still searching for that elusive something. Over the course of mining for my passion I've spent a scary amount of money pursuing what I hoped would be "my thing". What I learned is that the amount of money expended is not directly proportional to the pleasure derived.

In my thirties I was sure that if I bought a good tennis racket, the proper shoes and a cute outfit, I would soon be challenging Chrissie Everett. Instead, I discovered that I'm not the least bit competitive and couldn't care if I hit the ball or not. When I acquired my grandmother's piano, I was convinced that after a few lessons I would be pounding the keys like Jerry Lee Lewis. Never happened. Buying a lovely down-filled Ditrani ski suit and ski equipment failed to make me love standing at the top of a hill freezing my knockers off. I've tried oil painting, pastels and watercolours. Pilates? I fell off my exercise ball and split my chin open. Yoga? Couldn't get the breathing straight. I was always inhaling when I should have been exhaling and exhaling when I should have been inhaling. And running hurts my brain with all that pounding.

I've taken golf lessons and tennis lessons. Most of my girlfriends love golf and have encouraged me to get involved and have convinced me I'm missing something. I find it excruciatingly boring. After three holes I'm ready to slit my wrists. It's hard to be passionate about something you're not good at and I want my natural aptitudes to kick in and make me a passionate participant immediately. Is that asking too much? Where oh where can my passion be? Is there a test I can take?

One thing I am sure of is that there is nothing I would rather be doing than reading a book, a magazine, a newspaper or even the French side of a cereal box. Words upon words linked together satisfy me like nothing else, except maybe a pot of tea and fresh brownies. But it's such a passive use of time that I feel "underemployed". I can't shake the guilt feelings when I spend an afternoon engrossed in a book or culling my pile of magazines. My inner voice keeps reminding me I should be doing something more productive, like running half-marathons, upping my heart rate in a Zumba class or at the very least doing my kegels.

Blogging satisfies my urge to write though I can't imagine ever writing a novel. Dialogue, characters and plot are not my forté. But blogging requires no prearranged show-up time, special clothes or financial outlay. I do it to clear my head of mental clutter. No deadlines. No editors. No agents. No explanations. Just me, my keyboard and those wonderful people who chose to follow what I have to say.

I'll never be competitive, athletic or particularly productive. But I think my passion lies in enjoying what I never had time for during my working life when I was constantly required to be competitive and productive. I'm passionate about my relationships with the people in my life. I'm a passionate and voracious reader. And I'm passionate about blogging. There's nothing I would rather be doing than reading and writing.

Have you found your passion? Is it community work, spirituality, entertaining, gardening? Enjoy your gift. We all have at least one.

Feeling uninspired? Take a nap

Leah Eichler's recent Women@Work column in The Globe and Mail was a source of inspiration and affirmation better than most I've read in a while. Eichler maintains that we often get our best ideas when our brains are off-duty. Haven't you ever been struck with a brilliant idea just as you're about to drop off to sleep or when you're walking the dog through the park? According to Eichler we should give ourselves more down-time to allow these bursts of inspiration to emerge. Research has shown that we need quiet time for our brains to arrive at the state of Zen conducive to new ideas.

I agree wholeheartedly. For that reason, I keep a pad and pencil on my night table and another in the map pocket of my car so I can write down these flashes of genius when they happen, or at the next red light. Fortunately I'm very good at zoning out. And to think teachers used to yell at us for not paying attention. Just think of all the earth-shattering discoveries and inventions they probably killed when we were daydreaming in school.

Multi-tasking and "busyness" are considered virtues in today's world of 24/7 cell phones, e-mail and texting. All this hyperactivity is ultimately counter-productive. Thomas Edison would regularly sit on his boat dock holding a fishing pole and line in the water, with no bait. He needed time to think. Bill Gates used to isolate himself at his cottage for a week to free his mind for creativity. Gordon Lightfoot would check into a hotel and stay in his room for days to be free from distractions so he could write songs. And, Winston Churchill is well-known for his afternoon power naps that freed his mind from the stresses of trying to save the world from destruction.

When I was working, I always found the activity and noise inherent in daily office life to be distracting. My best ideas always came when I was doing some non-work-related activity. I needed my head to be free of clutter and my brain to be in a happy place to be truly productive.

So, with that in mind, please excuse me while I go take a nap. There are major world problems that need solving and I'm pretty sure I'm just on the cusp of finding the cure for the common cold—right after I summon up that Nobel-prize-worthy literature bubbling away in there somewhere. Maybe checking into a Four Seasons Hotel in Bali with the scent of fragrant blossoms and the sounds of surf outside my window would help. It certainly can't hurt.

I'm not okay . . . are you okay?

Could the once-brilliant minds of our entire Boomer generation be slowly slip-sliding away? Was it too much wine and other mood-enhancers? Do we have late-onset brain damage from all those years of sleeping on brush rollers in high school? Or are we retiring too early and "losing it"? Perhaps the sins and excesses of our youth are coming home to haunt us. In a short twenty-four-hour span this past weekend I experienced and witnessed enough lapses in cognition to cause major concern.

It began on Friday when I joined a girlfriend for lunch at her condo. The table was beautifully set with fine china, colourful, origami-folded napkins, a little gift bag at each place and large goblets for our flavoured mineral water (if we drink wine at lunch we fall asleep before dessert). When I questioned the third place-setting and my hostess mentioned it was for so-and-so, I reminded her that so-and-so had e-mailed a week earlier that she couldn't come. OMG. Hostess didn't read the entire e-mail and just assumed the reply was an acceptance. On the positive side, that meant that I could gorge myself silly on extra finger sandwiches and fruit flan.

The second misadventure was a double-header. When my honey and I got married, the wedding date conveniently corresponded closely with his birthday so he'd have no excuse for forgetting our anniversary. Anniversary on the twelfth, birthday on the sixteenth – simple. On the morning of the twelfth I gave him his birthday present and cards and wished him a happy birthday. "But it's not my birthday" he said. Second OMG! "Oh no. You're right. Today's not your birthday, it's our anniversary" I yelled as I snatched the gift and cards from his hands. "It's our *anniversary?*" he replied. Emergency run to Superstore for flowers and card. We'd both screwed up. The honeymoon's over.

About an hour later, we received a phone call from friends who'd gone to another friend's cottage for the weekend. After taking a day off work on Friday and driving four hours to get to the cottage, they arrived to find no-one there—they'd got the date wrong and were a week early! Another four-hour drive and they're back in the city and miraculously, still married.

Other friends were scheduled to meet for dinner in a restaurant. The first couple arrived on time and when their friends had not arrived after an hour of waiting, they e-mailed pictures of their empty plates with comments, "We're hungry. Where are you?" Oops! They were a week early.

Finally, on Saturday we went to my husband's birthday celebration (on our anniversary, in case you're having trouble keeping all this straight) at his son's place in London, Ontario. During the late-afternoon cocktail and munchies fest, his grandson asked my husband what type of car he should buy. Puzzled by the question, said grandson produced a blank cheque I had written for said grandson's birthday. In the course of writing a number of birthday and graduation gift cheques I had inadvertently neglected to fill in the amount. Thank God no one at Canada Post was having a bad day and intercepted that one or we'd be living in our car and getting paper routes to keep us in Pinot Grigio.

Calendar confusion? Inattention to detail? What's next? It wasn't that long ago I used nail polish remover instead of toner on my face when I inadvertently picked up the wrong bottle. What if I mistake a tube of bathtub grout for my retinol cream? How long will it be before I start hiding my own Easter eggs? Has the Mad Men/Mad Women era finally arrived—literally? I'm *not* okay with that. Are you?

The age of acquisition . . .
Too much of a good thing

The other day a friend mentioned that she was having a hard time picking out a new washer and dryer as her old ones had crapped out. With the profusion of choices available it was all so confusing—front loader, top loader, steam feature, stacking or pedestal? Then there are the hundreds of models, manufacturers, price options and warranty issues to sort out. In a less costly version of the same scenario, I stood in front of the hair conditioner section in the drug store the other day and felt faint when confronted with hundreds of bottles of varying sizes, colours and claims that basically all do the same thing. If I make the wrong choice will I wake up bald? Our range of choices for material and consumer goods in today's market is obscene. Sadly, I am as guilty of being sucked into the materialism vortex as anyone.

I heard on the radio that a recent study concluded that people are more positively affected and left with longer-term feelings of happiness as a result of *experiences* rather than *things*. A girlfriend once planned to buy her mother a silver tea service for her sixty-fifth birthday, something her mother had always wanted. When she ran the idea past her mother she was surprised by the response. "I wanted it when I was younger" she said "but now I realize it's not important and I really don't want to be bothered polishing it." I think we now understand the significance of this.

As Boomers get older we also get a bit smarter (quelle suprise!). We are now reaching a point in life where we're lightening our load, or at least trying to. We're looking for smaller, more efficient houses or condos. We're hauling bags of clothes and household goods to Good Will and keep promising ourselves we'll stop impulse buying. Trips to the mall are fraught with temptation to buy more crap we do not need and have no room for. When I find myself lusting after some cute top in a store or a gorgeous pair of shoes, I find I'm now realizing that I probably already have something almost like it at home.

I have more white blouses, black sweaters and black pants than I'll ever need for the rest of my life. As a teenager in the early sixties I owned one good white blouse —a hand-me-down from a friend. I wore that blouse to death. I clearly remember washing it by hand on a Saturday morning, hanging it outside on the clothesline, bringing it in to iron it and wearing it still damp (we didn't own a clothes dryer) in the afternoon to meet my girlfriend for our Saturday afternoon Coke fix, the old-fashioned kind that comes out of a fountain and can be flavoured with cherry, vanilla, chocolate, maple or strawberry syrup.. Today I probably have no less than a dozen white blouses. How far I've fallen?

One of my weaknesses is magazines and I subscribe to eighteen per month, which get recycled to girlfriends. But all that advertising suggesting that I could have better, shinier hair, smoother skin, more fashionable clothes, longer, thicker eyelashes, a thinner body and a more rewarding lifestyle is downright depressing. My mind is being bombarded with too many choices which make choosing anything a stressful endeavor. And the message that I am not good enough as I am is not only wrong, it's destructive.

Perhaps we've now reached the point my friend's mother reached about the silver tea set. Most things being promoted as the key to eternal happiness, I don't need, no longer want and don't want to maintain. The things I truly enjoy the most are *experiences* that cost next to nothing. For example:

1. Sitting drinking multiple cups of tea while I read The Globe and Mail in the morning and not having to watch the clock to rush off to work. I'm retired.

2. Getting together with friends.

3. Sitting outside in the shade reading my books and magazines with my little dog on my lap.

4. Having a conversation with my husband about whatever and anything and having my husband to share my life.

6. Sliding into nice fresh outside air-dried sheets at the end of the day in good health and reading some more.

7. And I love blogging. I even managed to get my internet provider to lower my monthly service fee because I'm not a huge consumer of data bytes.

I'm so happy that one of *your* choices was to read my blog—and it didn't cost you a thing or add clutter to your home. Thank you for reading "mes pensées" whoever and wherever you are.

Art and music in perfect harmony

Normally I don't even open the touchy-feely e-mails that frequent our in-boxes, but something about this one made me double-click. It's Don Maclean singing his famous song from 1971 written as a tribute to Vincent Van Gough, after reading his biography. I had not realized the source of inspiration for the song and it now touches me in a way not previously realized. Skip the ad at the beginning. Enjoy.
http://www.youtube.com/watch?v=PsxfvwuCqxo

To all the men I've loved before

Valentine's Day prompted me to reflect on the gift of love. One of the pitfalls of young love is our tendency to focus so much of our devotion on our new love that we lose ourselves in the process. It's a relationship hazard stemming from lack of experience. After you've done this once or twice, you get smart and realize you're actually a pretty cool person in your own right. I once dated a trucker who had the bad-boy swagger and looks of a young Jack Nicholson. Before I knew it, I was going to country and western bars, drinking beer and smoking Export A's. While liking country music is not a bad thing, some of the other behaviours I adapted to be "closer" to him were not so admirable. And he ran with a group of very unsavoury friends.

Later on, I dated a successful businessman who had three teenagers who were perhaps the most spoiled, ungrateful individuals I'd ever met. He was a single father to the three of them and I suppose to compensate for the fact their mother had left (who can blame her) he allowed them to manipulate him shamelessly. For the sake of the relationship I pretended I liked them which was a mistake. I should never have invested time in a relationship with a guy whose values were so divergent from my own.

The other night I watched a rom-com movie called Fever Pitch starring Drew Barrymore and Jimmy Fallon. The premise is based on

Barrymore's character adapting to the Fallon character's all-consuming love of baseball to the point she becomes exhausted, frustrated and bitter. It perfectly illustrates the pitfalls of burying our authentic selves to further the relationship at the expense of our authentic selves.

One of the greatest benefits of getting older is the advantage of hindsight. We can look back on the compromises we made in the name of love that were not aligned with who we really are. Getting older is getting smarter. That includes not bending our personalities to satisfy the people we think we love. This is not the same thing as compromising on smaller issues for the sake of keeping the peace or accepting minor differences. For example, my husband loves golf. I find it excruciatingly boring. I love words and writing which is anathema to him. I'll never "get" football but I have no problem with him watching it twenty-four-seven as long as I don't have to listen to it, which is why headphones are marriage-savers. Accepting and appreciating our inherent differences can actually enrich a relationship when you don't expect your partner to be your everything. That's unrealistic. It is fun sharing your common interests and fun sharing stories about things you do not have in common. Having differences of opinion is natural. Bending your basic makeup to always be the same as your partner's is not.

In earlier times when lifespans were shorter, people generally died before they racked up forty years of marriage. Nowadays, it's not uncommon for couples to divorce after twenty or thirty years when they come to the realization they may have compromised themselves for the sake of the relationship and that's not the way they want to spend the remaining thirty or more years of their lives.

And our criteria for an optimal mate change over the years. When we're in our twenties we want a cute guy with a sense of humour who's a good dancer. In our sixties we want a healthy guy with a sense of humour and a good RRSP.

Spending the rest of your life with someone who encourages the best in you is infinitely more agreeable than living out your years with someone who expects you to sell your soul. Life is precious, particularly your own. Loving another person is beautiful but loving yourself first is the first step. Happy Valentine's Day my loves!

Reflecting on what might have been

So much of what happens in our lives turns on the smallest decisions we make along the way. When confronted with a fork in the road we often give little thought to whether we go left or right but even the simplest decisions can dramatically affect the course of our entire lives. Or, as often happens the choices are not in our hands, such as a tragic car accident.

Have you ever thought about what your life would be like today if you'd made a different choice many years ago or if events had taken a different turn? While this is a shell game of sorts, I prefer to look on my own forks in the road from a positive perspective. A lot of my reflections on these hypothetical situations arise from my relationships with guys I thought I loved when I was young.

At the ripe age of nineteen I was sure I wanted to marry my boyfriend at that time who was sweet, kind and hardworking. As it happens, I moved on and he married someone else not long after. He was not a complicated or professionally ambitious person and only wanted to have a decent job, get married and have a family. Tragically, he had a stroke at the age of twenty-one that left him paraplegic and confined to a wheelchair for the rest of his life. His then-wife left him.

A couple of years later I thought I was in love and wanted to marry someone I met while traveling in Europe on my Eurailpass. He was in the American military stationed in Germany during the height of the Vietnam War in 1967-68. A few days in Paris with someone tall, dark and handsome at an age when your hormones are in overdrive is hardly a sensible time to be making life-altering decisions. If I'd married him, I'd be living in a depressed suburb of Detroit today as the wife of a retired or layed-off Ford assembly-line worker – if I'd stuck it out, which is highly unlikely. Later on, I almost married an abusive womanizer and that possibility still fills me with horror.

When I left school, I worked for Bell Telephone for six years until one day I impulsively left at noon and told them I wouldn't be back. I have certainly never regretted that move. Later on I worked for a much more progressive company that gave me the opportunity to soar. Or what about the decision I made at the age of forty to not have a child as a single mother. I'll never know whether I really made the right decision about that one, and even though I look around me at problems faced by friends with grown children and grandchildren, I'm still wistful about the direction I chose.

Many years later my entire life took a complete one-hundred-and-eighty degree turn in one evening when I accepted an invitation to dinner with my current husband whom I'd known for thirty years at the time. Never imagining the outcome, it was a life-changing event. A friend met her husband in Sierra Leone when his plane was diverted there while enroute to Biafra for a CUSO volunteer mission more than forty years ago. That single decision by the pilot during the flight changed both their lives forever.

Life is a series of such twists and turns and while we will never know what might have been, one thing I'm sure of is that those choices and their consequences are what make us the interesting, multi-faceted people we are today. We have a few miles on us. Some choices might have been better but even the poor choices are enriching for their lessons learned. When I hear people wish to regain their youth and so-called glory days, I'm shocked. I wouldn't want to go back even a day. As the old saying goes, we're still on the right of the sod and it doesn't get any better than that.

It is written, therefore it is . . . retained

Albert Einstein was once asked a simple question for which he did not have the answer. The world-renowned genius' response was, "I don't clutter my head with things that can be found in a book." I knew there was a reason that story has stayed with me. And I certainly don't clutter my head with anything I can do without.

The journal Psychological Science reports that tests on university students who hand-wrote their class notes instead of typing them on a laptop had better retention of what they were learning. The Cleveland Browns of the NFL have put this knowledge to practical use and now require that their players write team strategies by hand. According to Dr. Daniel J. Levitin, author of Organized Mind, professor and neuroscientist at McGill University in Montreal, our brain has only so much capacity for retained information so we should not clutter it with useless information. The human brain works much like our laptops. We have ROM for functioning and RAM for storing data and I certainly wouldn't like my RAM to jam. It might affect my ROM and then I'd be royally screwed.

On an everyday level we can all relate to the importance of "To Do" lists in our lives. If we write down a task and enjoy the act of stroking it out when it's completed, we feel satisfied and less stressed.

Taking this a step further, Dr. Levitin suggests that making "To Do" lists is a kind of mental clutter that should be dispensed with in favour of breaking down the tasks. We should put each task or piece of information on a separate piece of paper such as an index card to free the brain from what he calls "rehearsal loop" or replaying of an idea or task repeatedly to remember it. Students practise this technique by writing and rewriting information on flash cards or index cards to etch it in their brains for exams. Stupid me—I just tried to memorize everything and was rewarded with dismal results.

However, maybe I have genius potential after all. A few years ago, after I retired I ditched my "To Do" list system in favour of putting sticky Post-In notes on my kitchen cupboard doors. After I complete the *ironing* sticky note, I gleefully rip it off and stash in the drawer for reuse next time. This system works beautifully and keeps me organized and stress-free. Perhaps Dr. Levitin would like to research my brain. I'm amazing at retaining garbage but have trouble remembering the simple sequence of the three buttons I need to push on the remote to engage my PVR. Fortunately, I wrote it down on a stickie that I keep beside the remote. Otherwise my life would be chaos. Now it's Guide, Record, Select. Simple, but I can only retain that information as long as it's written on a yellow stickie. It's genius.

Chapter 5
Body

You Make Me Feel Like a Natural Woman
. . . Aretha Franklin, 1968

The joy of menopause
The honest-to-goodness truth

Last week as I was watching Bill Maher on HBO, he invited author, speaker and performance artist Sandra Tsing Loh to join the panel at the half-way point in the show. This is often when the new guest has a book to promote. More than once I've enjoyed this part of the show so much I've gone on-line and ordered the book immediately and that's exactly what happened when I downloaded Tsing Loh's The Madwoman in the Volvo on to my Kindle before the show was even over.

Subtitled My Year of Raging Hormones, the book describes Loh's midlife struggle with combining motherhood, overseeing an aging father, a marriage breakup and new relationship and depression while entering that dicey time of life known as menopause. She describes her daily life in terms any working woman can relate to, such as, driving children to various functions in the midst of domestic chaos, stressing about work deadlines, trying to keep a marriage viable with creative meals and date nights and coping with a difficult aging parent. Loh's situation is further complicated by having two children who are still in elementary school at an age when most women are seeing their progeny off to college. She finds herself ill-equipped to deal with the noise, the demands and the sheer physical energy required to keep all the plates spinning while she's experiencing hot flashes, depression, anger, resentment and loss of libido.

As I started reading I found myself thinking, "This is just another one of those books about how life is demanding, not always rewarding and sometimes you just want to give up. Ho hum, nothing different here." What makes this book different and so incredibly special is her stark honesty about her shortcomings and coping mechanisms. We can sympathize and empathize with her often hilarious descriptions of dealing with her eighty-eight-year old Chinese father's issues and the day-to-day challenges of family, work and marriage. Things really picked up in the latter half of the book where she looks deeper into the harsh truths about her own makeup and how she turns things around. She exposes her barnacles and gives us permission to do whatever works for each of us to get rid of them and find our joy. From the halfway point the book just gets better, moving with a nice rhythm, picking up speed and climaxing at the end in a wonderful multiple orgasms of wisdom and support. It's almost as if you should read the book from back to front.

Happily, The Madwoman in the Volvo is not encumbered with pages and pages of footnotes and bibliography material. It is not a rehash of other people's research and studies. The only major book she references is Dr. Christiane Northrup's The Wisdom of Menopause, which is universally read and respected as the definitive word on menopause issues. Loh's book is a wonderfully subjective, humorous recounting of her own experience and recommendations. We are not told to choke down eight glasses of icky green liquid every day, punish our bodies with yoga and Pilates or live on a diet of steamed kale, broccoli and boiled chicken. In fact, trying to add these disciplines to our already-busy lives can often add to our stress levels when we're barely holding ourselves together.

One of the most interesting things I learned is that our estrogen-fuelled years between puberty and menopause are actually the "unusual" years because we are pumped up with a temporary supply of high-octane hormones (estrogen, progesterone) to cope with mating, child-bearing, mothering, and nurturing. When we hit menopause, our hormone levels actually return to where they were before puberty so we are in fact once again our authentic selves. That's why she maintains there's nothing wrong with telling the kids to make their own lunch, leave home or simply grow up. She gives us permission to get more sleep, hire help around the house if we want to and treat ourselves with a little TLC. Don't beat yourself up because you're a few pounds overweight – remember, we didn't have waistlines when we were ten years old either. After all those years of putting everyone else first, menopause brings us back to square one where it's natural and not unhealthy to make ourselves a priority. Isn't that wonderful? No need to feel guilty. We're vindicated. Girlfriend—you nailed it. I'd give Madwoman in the Volvo ten out of ten.

Men can help prevent cervical cancer

When Baby Boomers came of age and the sexual revolution began, we could thank the pharmaceutical industry for introducing the birth control pill at just the right time.

No longer faced with the prospect of an unwanted pregnancy, Boomers embraced free love. In retrospect we were also an extremely lucky generation. Sexually transmitted diseases were not as rampant as they are today. Most STDs were treatable and not life-threatening. Today, anyone with an active sex life is also faced with the horror of AIDS and more than forty varieties of Human Papilloma Virus (HPV) as well as dozens of other STDs that may not be preventable, even with the use of condoms.

Fortunately the pharmaceutical industry has come through once more with a vaccine (Gardasil) that has the potential to prevent most HPV infections, a leading cause of cervical cancer. If I were young and not in a monogamous relationship I'd be first in line to get jabbed with the vaccine. If I had a son or daughter I'd encourage them to do the same thing—and hepatitis as well. What a gift. I'm not a health care expert but the prospect of preventing this horrible and incurable disease is a no-brainer.

In a discussion with a girlfriend the other day, I asked whether her twenty-something son had been vaccinated. The question caught her off-guard. As a conscientious mother she had never considered this risk before. It's a fact that guys/men can be unwitting transmitters of HPV without displaying any symptoms. And condoms do not entirely protect against the virus.

The May 2014 issue of Zoomer Magazine had an excellent article about the proliferation of sexually transmitted diseases among Baby

Boomers as well as in seniors already in extended living and other retirement facilities. The article describes actor Michael Douglas' struggle with throat cancer that was caused by an HPV virus passed through oral sex that remained dormant in his body for years. Just because we got off lucky in our younger days doesn't mean we don't need to be vigilant now. Men can be oblivious carriers of infection and as women we face the prospect of devastating cervical cancer if we're not careful.

As a mother, grandmother, aunt or friend, please encourage not only the women but also the males in your life to investigate with their doctor their role in prevention. Not only is it the gentlemanly thing to do, it could save the life of a female you love. Prevention of cervical cancer is not just a women's issue. And prevention of HPV could prevent the men in your life from getting throat cancer.

Don't let stress be the end of you

We've all felt our blood pressure rising when we step behind someone with a cart full of groceries in the ten-items-or-less *Express* aisle. Or when someone zips into the parking spot you've sat patiently waiting for. Yesterday I spent forty minutes trying to sort out a tech problem on the phone with a call centre only to have the line suddenly go to dial tone, with my problem unresolved. These frustrations are minor, however, compared to the ongoing or prolonged stress associated with financial problems, chronic illness, childhood trauma, an abusive spouse or job pressures and job loss. Some people cope amazingly well in stressful situations while others worry excessively, lose sleep and use various coping methods such as drinking, abusing drugs or over-eating. While each of us manages stress in our lives differently, the insidious effects are cumulative and at a certain point our bodies scream for help.

Perhaps you know someone who pushes themselves too hard and before long they're sick with a cold or something worse. Stress takes an enormous toll on our immune systems consuming a great deal of energy that could have been diverted to more positive outcomes. Women are particularly vulnerable because we have been conditioned to put everyone else first. Even when we're feeling unwell or tired, we push through, going to work, preparing meals, chauffeuring children to activities, caring for husbands. Taken to the extreme this can seriously compromise our immune systems leading to temporary or chronic illness.

During my last few years of working, the effects of a high-pressure job combined with aging and changes in my personal life led to some health issues. A series of tests revealed that my cortisol levels (a stress hormone released by the adrenal gland) were more than three times the high-end of normal. As a result of that and in order to stop the health problems from getting worse, I decided to retire early.

A friend who has recently developed a number of health-related problems found her symptoms largely disappeared when she was on vacation and returned with a vengeance when she returned to work and the real world. Her doctor wisely suggested treatment for the psychological as well as physiological symptoms. That included watching a video by Vancouver Doctor Gabor Maté that is available on You-Tube. I'm sharing the link here and you may see yourself or someone you know described in the video. It takes nearly an hour but is well worth the time. Listen to your body's signals and take care of yourself—before it's too late.

Check out: http://www.youtube.com/watch?v=c6IL8WVyMMs

Olive oil – the real deal

Italy has been waging a war on fake olive oils with limited success but I came across some information that may be helpful to consumers to ensure we're getting certified genuine extra virgin olive oil – not a facsimile that has been diluted with canola oil or who knows what else. Check out this website to bring yourself up to speed on the real deal. http://truthinoliveoil.com/. You can't always trust labelling.

Now I have to worry about my liver too

The liver is a very important organ and one I always took for granted – assumed because it didn't hurt and everything else seemed to be ticking along, we were in good shape. Not necessarily so. Sometimes it just doesn't pay to read the newspaper or watch the news on television. The news just gives me something else to worry about and I consider worrying a useless, wasteful expenditure of energy.

A seventeen-year old boy was recently given emergency treatment for liver failure at Texas Children's Hospital. The source of his illness, a concentrated green tea extract purchased at a nutrition store as a "fat-burning" supplement! The boy was put on the waiting list for an immediate liver transplant. We're often being warned by various sources to be extremely cautious about using so-called health supplements and herbal remedies. Like pet food, there are no federal controls on health supplement ingredients. The packaging does not legally have to list all ingredients, and toxicity may be a crap shoot. That just makes me want to go and toss all my supplements including my calcium, my fish oils and everything else.

As a pet owner, I'm always vigilant about what I feed my three-pound Yorkie, particularly since friends of ours lost their beloved Shih Tzu to kidney failure caused by dried chicken tender treats that falsely proclaimed "one hundred percent chicken product" on the package. I recently e-mailed Purina about the contents of their "DentaStix" to see if a) they were a product of a foreign country, and b) were any of the ingredients from off-shore? I can only take their lack of response as bad news.

Do we really have to start growing our own non-genetically-modified fruit and veggies? Meat is already a highly suspect product. And now, a simple cup of tea might be a killer. Next time I go to the doctor, I'm going to get my liver checked. It's not enough to monitor my heart, blood pressure, cholesterol, body fat, lungs, bones and female organs, now I have to add my liver to the list. On one hand we're lucky to have the monitoring tools available to keep us healthy but it's not without its downside. The work never ends.

Step right up and look twenty years younger

Boomer Broads have been warned from an early age to take care of our skin, like French women do. Use sunblock, cleanse, tone, moisturize. There are serums for tightening, serums for lightening, serums for plumping, serums for smoothing – serums for everything. Cosmetics companies, estheticians and dermatologists are making billions of dollars feeding our insecurities.

I have invested the cost equivalent of a luxury German car in skincare products and I still have acne, rosacea, itching, blotching and bumping. Those glossy ads in magazines are so seductive. Every new skincare product promises to deliver perfect smooth skin.

There's a cupboard in our bathroom which serves as medicine cabinet, drugstore, beauty supply outlet and fountain of youth. I purchased extra shelves to accommodate my copious supplies of makeup, hair care products, skin care potions, nail polishes including top coats, base coats, cuticle creams, nail strengtheners and buffers clippers, emery boards and files, hair brushes, rollers and combs, cotton pads, sun blocks, fake tanners, cleansers, toners, moisturizers, primers, peelers, plumpers, body creams, foot creams, exfoliators, clippers, sanders, pluckers and lash curlers. Each item is a necessary ingredient in getting me through the day. My husband owns a razor, antiperspirant, and hairbrush which occupy less than five inches of space at the front of one shelf.

Every month the fashion and beauty magazines introduce more new miracle creams, serums, lotions and cleansers. And every month I have to restrain myself from running out and buying the newest, latest and greatest. Standing in a drug store or the cosmetics section of a department store is not only bewildering and overwhelming it's just plain scary. If I don't buy into their dogma will I turn into the Sea Hag? I'd much rather face the day looking like Cameron Diaz than Keith Richards.

Watching makeup artists and beauty consultants on TV or reading their advice in magazines has become strangely amusing. Each one assumes a knowledgeable air and claims their expert advice is the definitive word on lip plumping, cheek sculpting or creating a smoky eye.

Many years ago I worked for a major cosmetics company selling their products in a swanky downtown Toronto department store. I too assumed a confident air while I assured my customers that the one hundred and twenty-five dollar night cream would most definitely make their dreams come true. In fact, I knew nothing more about it than they did. It's all about hope. And let's not forget that all those pictures of perfect complexions and thick hair in magazines have been Photo-shopped to crazy extremes to depict the ideal.

And now they've thrown Botox, fillers and expensive surgical procedures into the mix. Should I? or Shouldn't I? Or would I rather take a trip to Paris with the money? Or perhaps save it for my retirement? Or pay my mortgage? There isn't a woman on TV or in the movies anymore who is capable of moving her forehead or upper lip – their faces are paralyzed to look like wax. How is that a good thing?

The October 2013 issue of MORE Magazine had the results of their 2013 beauty search among women "of a certain age". One of the winners, Evelyn Harris, age seventy-one has lovely silver hair combed back in a stylish bob and she has beautiful skin. Her secret? "I've washed my face with Dial soap most of my life, and I use a little Aquaphor on dry spots on my skin. I've never had plastic surgery and I let my silver hair grow in years ago, in my forties" she says. Coincidently, when I joined Ma Bell in 1965, as part of my medical examination at hiring, they suggested I wash my face with Dial soap.

Now I understand that today's cosmetics are supposedly far superior scientifically to what we had even a year ago, but it's hard to argue with the evidence. My mother is eighty-four years old and does not have a wrinkle. Her skin is like porcelain. Her beauty regimen? Fifty years of Dove soap and Nivea Crème. Who's the smart one here? Is it nature or nurture? Darned if I know? Oops. Gotta go. The Oil of Olay tank truck just pulled up.

Man cannot live by meat alone

Men love their meat. My husband and two of his friends, Dan and Dave (names changed to protect the guilty) are off for a testosterone-packed weekend closing down Dan's cottage on a lake north of Gananoque, Ontario. The last two days have been a whirl of preparations involving grocery lists, wardrobe consultations and beverage inventories. Dan e-mailed a copy of the food plan that confirmed there's not a sprig of kale in sight. Here it is and I'm not making this up:

Friday Lunch: Hamburgers

Friday Dinner: Beer Can Chicken

Saturday Breakfast: Bacon & Eggs

Saturday Lunch: Cold Cuts

Saturday Dinner: Steak & Potatoes

Sunday Breakfast: Egg McMuffins

And don't tell Dave's wife. She's a registered dietician and he's had heart surgery.

Happy as clams they were as they set off at six o'clock in the morning for their he-man trek to the hinterland in Dan's shiny new Lincoln. A cell phone call when they arrived revealed that a strong windstorm had knocked out the electricity so they were roughing it with only a fireplace and wood stove until the power came back on. The immediate plan was to head into the bush to forage for a nice full-bodied Brunello. When the chest-thumping stops and the hydro returns, I should have more to report.

Follow up: With the power out on Friday evening, our resourceful outdoorsmen prepared the beer-can chicken on the barbecue illuminated by a flashlight held in the mouth of the cook. In order to withstand the rigors of life on an island without electricity, copious amounts of above-mentioned Brunello and whatever other swill they could get their hands on was consumed to stave off the cold and demands of the elements. This resulted in an early bedtime but that's okay because early-to-rise is the order of the day in the Canadian wilderness and they just can't party like they used to.

Saturday morning bacon and eggs was followed by a boat ride to the mainland and a cross-country trek to town in the trusty Lincoln to hunt for more meat. Dan's sons and friends had arrived to build the foundations for a new Bunkie. As any woodsman knows, a barn-raising is hard work and always requires extra food and libation to fortify the volunteers.

On the way back to the camp, they encountered a gigantic rock formation used by the Indians to mark a trading post of sorts. As they stealthily approached the native encampment, the flashing neon signs indicated they had discovered the Gananoque Thousand Island Casino, where they joined other traders and were promptly relieved of a large portion of their wampum.

The menfolk have now returned to civilization. Their return was delayed waiting for the dishwasher at the cottage to cycle off before blowing out the lines for winter – the demands of life in the bush. Happy to be home! Gotta' love 'em.

Hormones make the world go 'round

I have always maintained that if women ruled the world there would be no war. Women do not send their sons, brothers, husbands or lovers off to be killed or maimed in wars about power. We'd put the kettle on, make a nice pot of tea, put out some warm chocolate chip cookies and sort it out. It has to do with testosterone. Men have a lot more of it than women and as a result they do stupid things.

Take starting a business. When men decide to start their own business, they lease a Lexus, rent some swanky office space with a perky young receptionist, invite their cronies for expense-account lunches and wait for the business to pour in.

Women, on the other hand, set up a computer and phone on an IKEA desk in the basement, spare bedroom or dining room table and go to work – the hard way – writing a business plan, a marketing plan, and a financial plan. Then they start making calls, attend networking sessions and writing proposals, all while juggling daily chores like dropping off and picking kids up at school and/or daycare, grocery shopping, preparing meals, doing laundry, checking on aging parents and trying to fit in a pedicure once a month.

The difference in these approaches is hormonal. Testosterone makes men think they are better than they probably are. Their confidence is enhanced when they are arrayed in the requisite cock feathers of male success – a nice car, a generous expense account and the company of other alpha males. The yardstick by which many men measure success is numbers. The guy with the highest number wins.

- Dollar sign + highest number of digits in salary = Success
- Highest number of psi in a power washer = Success
- Most horsepower in car, outboard motor, lawn mower or snow blower = Success
- Highest number of penile inches = Success
- Most inches in big-screen TV = Success
- Most big-screen TVs = Success
- Of course golf scores are moot as they all lie anyway.

Women's numbers are different. *Smaller* numbers equal success. For example:

- Quick shower, put on makeup, feed kids, exit house in minimum time = Success
- Dropped six pounds on the scale this week = Success
- Fewest number of trips to grocery store per week = Success
- No lost socks in this week's laundry = Success
- Zero balance on this month's Visa bill = Success

- Finally fit into size eight jeans = Success
- Go to bed at 10:00 p.m. instead of midnight = Success
- Only two items left on today's "To Do" list = Success

Does this mean we should start slipping estrogen into men's morning coffee? Would the world really be a better place if they watched less TSN and more HGTV? Absolutely not! It's the differences that make us so interesting. Except for the bit about war; Obama, Putin, Morsi – put the kettle on. Have some brownies together.

Fed up with food

Canadian Broadcasting Corporation's *Fifth Estate* recently did a program on the evils of sugar that scared the crap out of me. And I keep reading about the horrific effects of my personal drug of choice, Diet Coke. Gluten is the current villain in the tricky world of food. Carbs are known killers, but who among us knows the difference between bad carbs and good carbs. Eat local. Eat seasonal. Coffee has rebounded from being a suspected carcinogenic to "some coffee is a good thing". Red meat is a reviled source of protein but we supposedly need some animal protein – although vegans and vegetarians will disagree with this.

My head is swimming with so many do's and don'ts about what I should and should not eat that it's hardly worth bothering anymore. The *Eat Right for Your Blood Type*, *Fit For Life*, *The Kind Diet*, *French Women Don't Get Fat*, *The Zone* and various other dictums offer conflicting and often just plain bad advice on how we should fuel our bodies. My bookshelves are sagging with dozens of books like this. Every time I see a new so-called expert promoting their "eat-your-way-to-good-health-and-live-forever" book I cover my eyes, plug my ears and make myself promise I won't get sucked in again. I'm going broke buying these books and the end result of trying to implement the various plans is nothing but stress and anxiety.

Thanks to the wisdom of a naturopath and Weight Watchers over the years, I have tracked my poisons to the nth degree and I'm sick and tired of the whole thing. I have a pretty fair idea of what is good and bad for me and every time I bite into a crispy piece of toast and jam or a nice fresh butter tart I'm filled with self-loathing. And I'm not alone. All my friends have also become carb-calorie-sugar-preservatives-GMO-watching vigilantes. And while we may live to be one hundred and fifty, we're not enjoying food anymore.

When I was growing up in small-town Ontario in the fifties, our family ate three meals a day – at home – breakfast, dinner (as the midday meal was called then) and supper. Today's lifestyles do not permit that kind of routine. Breakfast back then consisted of cereal and toast, usually with a cup of tea and small glass of orange juice. Supper was meat, potatoes, a vegetable and a dessert of homemade pudding, pie, cake or something similar and sweet. The midday meal was leftovers from the night before. Which means we ate potatoes twice a day, half the time fried in butter or bacon fat in a cast iron frying pan, and two desserts each day? Yet, we were all thin and fit. Like most families then, we never ate out in a restaurant. Fast food did not exist. Restaurants were luxuries. I'd never tasted pizza or Chinese food until I left home to move to Toronto at the age of seventeen to go to work.

Ironically, we still buy into the pet food companies' marketing dictates about only commercial dog food being suitable for our four-legged family members. Logically, if we humans should be eating only fresh, organic, locally-grown foods from each of the food groups, why would we feed our pets the cardboard processed kibble that passes as pet food? Even my little Yorkie knows a good thing when she sees it. I feed her half and half – processed commercial dog food mixed with good quality human food like carrots, chicken, steak, broccoli, fish oil etc. She cleverly separates the real food from the processed food eating only the human food and licking the exterior surface of the dog food clean but leaving it in her bowl. Who says dogs can't taste the difference. My girlfriend's farm dog even refused to eat the Kraft processed cheese slices she gave him. What does that say about our food supplies?

Today we have infinite choices in fresh, prepared, take-out and exotic foods. And a multi-billion dollar industry has been built around telling us what to eat and what to avoid. This steady barrage of food-related dogma has just plain worn me down. Think I'll go have a cup of tea and piece of banana bread and read my new book – *The Supercharged Hormone Diet*. That should make me feel better.

Scary Halloween faces

When I tuned in to *The Marilyn Denis Sh*ow a while ago I was shocked and horrified when Suzanne Somers was interviewed as Marilyn's guest. I've always admired Suzanne Somers' energy and resourcefulness but her face looked like she'd had a bad reaction to some kind of medication or had perhaps been stung by the world's largest bumble bee. And her neck was even worse than mine even though we're exactly the same age – sixty-six; swollen face and multiple neck folds – totally incompatible.

Why oh why do these women do this to themselves? Coincidently, I happened to see Patti Lovett-Reid on TV too. Patti is a Certified Financial Planner, a frequent media commentator on Baby Boomer financial issues and a former senior executive with TD Bank Financial Group. She's also a beautiful woman who appears to have done something unnecessary to her upper lip. Economist Sherry Cooper, Executive Vice-President and Chief Economist of BMO Financial Group, is another beautiful woman who has messed with a good thing and the result is not pretty.

I acknowledge that some people benefit greatly from these procedures. Somehow, they undergo fillers and Botox injections and still manage to look like a better version of themselves. Jane Fonda is an example of "good work." Unfortunately, others do not fare so well.

Every actress on TV these days seems to be unable to move her upper lip or "furrow her brow". Even Billy Crystal is looking weirdly altered. Why can't they just go the way of Audrey Hepburn who was still beautiful with her sixty-something face showing fine lines and wrinkles – and we could still see all of her beautiful natural smile with slightly crooked teeth, not just her bottom teeth below a frozen upper lip.

Smiles reveal iridescent glow-in-the-dark artificial veneers in Chicklet-straight rows.

It's always heartening to see public figures age gracefully. Before long, the movie and TV industries are going to be unable to find people to play grandmothers, senior citizens or even mothers who don't look from the neck up like they're only twenty-five years old. Although it could provide employment opportunities for Boomer Broads like me who still have all the lines and wrinkles consistent with our age and experience. The over-use of these procedures is scary. It's often unnecessary and frequently just plain wrong. The horror . . . . the horror.

Betty knows best

Betty White once said, "Why do people say, 'Grow some balls'? Balls are weak and sensitive! If you really want to get tough, grow a vagina! Those things take a pounding."

Creepy, crepey

The late Nora Ephron felt bad about her neck – she even wrote a book about it. I totally forgot about mine until it was too late. It happened overnight. When I was fifty-three I woke up one morning, looked in the mirror and was shocked to discover that my formerly long, lean neck now resembled a slouching sports sock. For years I had been dutifully applying hundreds or probably thousands of dollars' worth of creams, oils, serums and even stem cell potions to various parts of my body with reasonably good results but I forgot all about my neck. Just assumed it would always be what it was.

Since that initial shock several years ago, I've been trying to compensate, even beseeching the Goddess of Necks, Pernicious, to help me out but she's unforgiving. I've tried manipulating the folds by lifting, pulling and smoothing the offending area with my fingers. If I clipped a clothespin to a vertical section of flesh at the nape of my neck I appear as I once did, but unfortunately I would never be able to face anyone in profile or from the back. And that clothespin hurt. Surgery is just too scary and expensive and I don't want friends to know I'm that vain. I could become a Muslim and hide everything but my eyes under a veil. But then I could never visit Quebec or France. So I've decided I'll just put on a smile and pretend I don't notice – chin up, as they say.

Chapter 6
Causes

*United We Stand
. . . Brotherhood of Man, 1970*

My kinda' gun control

Oprah Magazine (http://www.oprah.com/omagazine) recently featured an article about a novel approach to gun control. The City of Newark, New Jersey joined forces with a jewelry designer to recycle the metals from guns collected during a paid gun amnesty program and create bracelets made from steel and brass gun parts. Each bracelet has the serial number of the gun inscribed on the edge. A portion of the profits produced from this program is returned to Newark to continue the program. The bracelets are available in three sizes for a custom fit and the one I bought fits perfectly. I currently have a steel one and plan to order a brass one as well.

The Caliber Foundation aims to offer support to victims and families of illegal gun violence. When a community is affected by gun violence there are many unforeseen and unplanned-for expenses, in the worst cases; funerals, and for those lucky enough to survive there are; medical bills, wheelchair ramps, and lost income. Churches and community organizations struggle to meet these needs, just as the Caliber Collection creates opportunities for those who may never have walked the streets of Newark to participate in making the city a safer place, the Caliber Foundation connects anyone who donates with the organizations and people on the front lines of re-building lives one small act at a time.

Every day in this country lives are lost, and hearts are broken, the Caliber Foundation offers a helping hand when it is needed, acts of generosity on the parts of many, to help families and communities heal and work together to change their Caliber.

I encourage you to support this program. Check it out at: www.jewelryforacause.net

A reminder to remember

"My kinda' gun control" was in support of a gun amnesty program in Newark, New Jersey that began under the leadership of Corey Booker. As the anniversary of the horror of Sandy Hook approaches, I think it is worth bringing the issue forward again.

The Caliber Foundation dismantles guns seized by police or surrendered during amnesty programs and recycles the metals to make jewelry. The rings, bracelets and necklaces are engraved with the serial number of the original weapon and proceeds from the profits are returned to support victims of gun violence and further amnesty programs.

This morning as I was half-watching The Today Show on TV, they described a similar venture that I think is worth mentioning. As a Canadian, it is easy to be self-righteous about the ubiquity of guns in the United States but we aren't without our own problems. The bottom line is we need to do whatever we can to reduce the number of guns in circulation. As ordinary citizens our options are limited to choosing not to own a gun and to support our police forces in their efforts to seize guns through these initiatives.

It's not too late to do a bit of Christmas shopping. Check out these websites and see if there is something you can order for your sweetie and/or yourself to support these efforts. www.libertyunited.com and http://www.jewelryforacause.net/caliber-foundation

I ordered the stainless steel bracelet from the Caliber Foundation a few months ago and was really happy with it. I've been meaning to order the matching brass one and now on the anniversary of Sandy Hook, I think it's time I did. Think about doing the same.

If women ran the world there would be no war

I cannot imagine a woman possessing the surge of testosterone required to push the button that brought down the civilian passenger airliner over the Ukraine or firing missiles at our neighbours. We would never send our loved ones off to kill other people to gain a bit of dirt. We'd put the kettle on and solve our differences over a nice cup of tea and plate of brownies. That premise got me thinking about what else would be different in the world if it were run by women. Here are a few possibilities to contemplate:

1. Governments would have balanced budgets and would be relatively debt-free, allowing for a minor misstep whenever summer shoes go on sale early. Federal budgets aren't that different in principle from personal budgets. We wouldn't need all those war toys to demonstrate how big our balls are. That money could be put to much better use for such things as daycare, healthcare and improved assistance for the truly poor.
2. All males would be required to pee sitting down. Enough said.
3. There would be no tailgating on the highways. Accidents would be greatly reduced with less speeding, lane-hopping and road-racing. Imagine how that would impact the insurance industry.
4. Fighting in hockey would be strictly forbidden. It would return to being a game of skill and endurance.
5. Those evil-minded Wall Street bankers would now be doing hard time and making restitution. Those who are left would have salaries and benefits capped, be required to do community service—and report to women.

6. Health care for everyone in the United States and other countries around the world would be a right, not a privilege enjoyed by the rich few.
7. Low-heeled comfortable shoes would be considered objects of beauty.
8. Useless calories and fat would be legislated out of all foods.
9. Weight and waist-line issues would be a thing of the past (see Item 8 above).
10. Older, mature women would be the most respected and revered members of our society for their wisdom, experience and inner beauty.
11. Wine, chocolate and bread would be declared health foods and would have no adverse effects.
12. Adult children would leave home at the age of eighteen and stay gone, forever, be financially independent and live happily ever after.
13. Affordable, convenient, quality daycare would be easily available for all parents.
14. All electronic equipment such as computers, tablets, Smart Phones, cable and satellite remote controls would be simple to use even for beginners, be voice activated and do exactly what we want them to do, without complications, errors, breakdowns and tantrums.
15. That unfortunate thing that happens to all women around the age of forty-eight to fifty would never transpire. We'd remain eternally wrinkle-free, slim, fit and dewey moist in all the right places, forever.

The possibilities are endless and intriguing. Imagine a world without wars, without borders (and the attendant customs duties), a world that is kind and nurturing, wise and wonderful. Many ancient societies were matriarchal including the early Egyptians and most indigenous people. Let's start by replacing Vladimir Putin with Elizabeth Warren as President of Russia.

John Lennon got it so right in his beautiful song, *Imagine*. Bette Midler echoed it in *From a Distance*. There would be no hunger. There would be no child abuse, no rape, no oppression of individuals due to gender, faith, economic status or nationality. Just imagine. .

We won the lottery

Being born in Canada with all its social benefits, economic stability, good manners and relatively boring politics is right up there with winning the lottery. It even partially compensates for our shitty winters. While we condemn our Prime Minister for his high-handed proroguing of parliament, at least our British-like system wouldn't stand for the disgraceful goings-on that are happening right now in the United States. They seem determined to internally combust. It's the old story of the tail wagging the dog and it's not a pretty sight.

We spend half the year in the United States and know that the current situation is definitely not the democracy preferred by the majority. The wheels have completely fallen off. In a country with some of the brightest people in the world, how can things go so far awry?

Please, Uncle Sam – play nice, share your toys, and stop bullying your friends and family. The current "time-out" isn't working and we hate to think what will happen next. It's not productive. As your neighbours we are very concerned.

Let them eat cake

Our sisters in public service have gone rogue and it's hurting not only our gender but the entire population. First it was Pamela Wallin, Beverley Hoda and now it's Alison Redford, former premier of Alberta and Susan Fennell, Mayor of Brampton. It seems that power is indeed intoxicating. Give a girl the keys to the castle and before long she's raiding the pantry. These Marie Antoinette wannabe's have brought shame on us all and I say off with their heads.

Every day new stories emerge of men and women who abuse their positions of trust and privilege in public service. Former Senators Mike Duffy and Patrick Brazeau have a list of misdeeds and illegal activities long enough to trip over. In a perfect world, the behavior of public servants should be above reproach. Their motives for seeking office should be noble and as taxpayers and citizens we should be able to trust them with the affairs of our country and the legitimacy of their expense accounts. Not so.

It's obvious the key to wealth and privilege is no longer winning the lottery. I've thrown thousands of dollars at that campaign already without success but fortunately I now have a guaranteed solution to financial security and possibly a paid-for full-time hairdresser. I'm going to run for Parliament in some safe little rural community like the one I grew up in half-way between Toronto and Ottawa. After a mere six years of representing the good people of that riding, I will be endowed with a full pension for life and lots of free travel benefits for me, my honey and my Boomer girlfriends. I get to attend free barbecues, ribfests and pancake breakfasts every weekend which means if I bring a bag I can take the leftovers home to eat for the rest of the week.

If I can sweet-talk the boss into making me a cabinet minister I also get a car and driver which means me and my girl posse can swill copious quantities of Ontario wine in the back seat of a limo without worrying about DUI issues. On special holidays I get to shake hands with the Duke and Duchess of Cambridge which certainly warrants a trip to Holt Renfrew (can I expense that? – who cares?)

Another benefit is that I actually only have to show up for work in the "House" for a few weeks each year. And all I'm required to do is periodically bang the desk with my perfectly manicured hand and wear a bright colour so my friends can see me on TV. I hear the members' cafeteria is, if not free, at least really cheap as it's subsidized by taxpayers. And I get a living allowance which means if I share accommodation with other porkers, I can pocket even more money for trips to Holts.

My heart beats faster just thinking about all the manna that would flow from being a public servant at the trough. And my mouth waters at the thought of all that free food, sixteen dollar glasses of freshly-squeezed orange juice that I don't have to pay for and the cases of Jackson-Triggs at my disposal. I only wish I'd thought of this forty years ago. I could have retired after "working" a mere six years. To pick up more money on the side and keep the gravy flowing, I could push for a set in the Senate.

So, my advice for Generation X and Y'ers who claim they can't get a job after spending all those years getting expensive degrees in Women's Studies, Sociology or Nineteenth Century Canadian Literature, run for Parliament. You'll be rolling in dough, have an unbelievable pension, tons of free time, unlimited Canadian wine and of course, yummy little free cakes. I can taste it now.

Buffalo Bills blow big-time

There is probably not another person on this planet who has less interest in or knowledge of football than I. From my vantage point it's simply a game of run, bump and fall down. Am I missing something? As I was listening to the *Ward & Al Show* on Canada Talks Sirius satellite radio the other day, however, I heard something that suddenly spiked my interest in the world of football immediately.

The Buffalo Bills who share a home team fan base with Toronto have a six-woman cheerleading squad called the Buffalo Jills. Five of the six members of the squad are suing the Bills' organization for unacceptable working conditions. This is where it gets interesting and I learned something I did not know. These women are not paid for their work nor are they reimbursed for expenses incurred in the performance of their responsibilities. Their love of football is supposed to suffice. Some of their complaints include having to pay from their own pockets for their six-hundred and fifty dollar "uniforms" for which they have to show receipts to verify that the uniforms are dry-cleaned at least once a month.

They are expected to attend numerous community and promotional commercial events for which they are not paid. They are not reimbursed for their travel and parking expenses for events or games in town or out-of-town. They are required to attend rehearsals three times a week and are subjected to "jiggle" tests to ensure they are maintaining a strict level of physical condition. There is an extensive list of requirements to be adhered to involving such things as personal hygiene, hair styles and even how often they must wash their feet. They are expected to sell calendars they have to pay for in advance and are not reimbursed for any they do not sell. And for all of this they are expected to be grateful for being allowed to see football games free and be groped.

This is a shameful, disgusting, unforgivable, indefensible, distressful, deplorable situation and the Buffalo Bills should be ashamed. Rarely have I heard of such exploitive work practices—and this from an organization worth billions of dollars that pays its players millions. Even the ticket collectors are treated better than the Buffalo Jills. Imagine the reaction if it were suggested the players not be compensated and be satisfied with the privilege and enjoyment of being part of the NFL. If the cheerleaders were male, fair wage and expense contracts would have been negotiated decades ago.

I understand this situation is not limited to just the Buffalo franchise. There is no doubt in my mind that the treatment of the cheerleaders is sexist and should never be tolerated. How many of the fans are aware of this situation and do they condone it? Would you let this happen to your daughter or granddaughter? If I didn't hate football already, I certainly have good reason to do so now. They have absolutely no concept of fair play and should be severely penalized.

Ce n'est pas possible
Proud Canadian stands corrected

Tristin Hopper, a reporter with The National Post has written an article challenging my claim in a recent blog (specifically Items three and eight) that Canadians are polite, decent and kind people. John Thompson, a Canadian and former director of Canadian Studies at North Carolina's Duke University cites many examples of Canadians behaving in very un-Canadian-like fashion in a variety of different locales and situations. Frankly, I'm shocked and appalled. Naturally, I attribute these abhorrent behaviours to younger generations who did not grow up with the strict disciplines familiar to Baby Boomers, such as corporal punishment in schools, going to bed without dinner and for other misdemeanors getting a smack up-side the head from your father when he got home. We soon learned to toe the line after a few wacks with the leather strap and sitting patiently through God-fearing sermons at church every single Sunday morning of our young lives.

Baby Boomers for the most part can be counted on to proudly wear our Maple Leaf pins when travelling in foreign countries without embarrassing fellow Canadians or our parents. We try to blend in, diligently trying to speak foreign languages and eating strange local foods without complaint. We do not raise our voices. We seek out local experiences and never demand burgers and fries.

In our defence, let's just say Rob Ford is merely on the cusp of being a Baby Boomer so we won't take responsibility for his bizarre behaviours in public. And I must agree with John Thompson that Canadian hockey fans can be belligerent, arrogant and downright nasty sometimes as can players and parents of players. It's a genetic fault we're not proud of. Justin Bieber is another one of the younger generation mentioned above who is currently doing us wrong.

Apparently the locals in vacation spots like the Dominican Republic and Mexico are not huge fans of Canadians either. Bellingham,

Washington residents resent Canadians swinging over the border from Vancouver to buy their cheap gas and dairy products and have threatened to have "Americans Only" days at the local Costco. While The National Post article did not specifically mention Florida, I have no doubt there are local Floridians who also find some Canadians less than loveable. It seems we often drink too much and get unruly when we're escaping our crappy winters in a warm southern climate.

Well now. This all comes as a huge disappointment to me. Maybe we should reinstate corporal punishment. And Rob Ford could most definitely afford to be sent to bed without dinner. Perhaps if we relaxed our archaic liquor laws, Canadians would not go wild and abuse alcohol when we're outside our borders.

My guy and I are planning a trip to France this fall and I promise we'll be on our best behaviour. If you spot us buying cheap gas to take back to Canada or ordering burgers and fries, please feel free to wack us up-side the head. We're going for the privilege of enjoying French hospitality while we visit World War I and II sites. We will drink all that wonderful wine in France and promise to leave behind anything we consume. I'll dazzle Parisians with my command of high school French. I'll be wearing my Canadian Maple Leaf pin and I won't embarrass my parents or fellow Canadians by appearing on the news as an obnoxious, drunk old Canadian lady demanding poutine on The Champs Elysées. Of this, you can be sure.

Giving women support where it counts

There's a little shop in downtown Cambridge, Ontario called WIGG (Women's International Gift Gallery) at 55 Dickson Street that is worth the drive to Cambridge. Affiliated with the YWCA, all proceeds from the shop are directed to providing sustainable programs that serve women and their families in the Cambridge community, and cultivate a society where women are respected, valued and equal.

Celebrity stylist Lynn Spence, who owns a home in Cambridge threw her support behind the shop recently by working in the store to help customers select and try on artsy clothes and jewelry from the selection sourced from around the world. Lynn presented a fashion show on CITY TV's *CityLine* to help showcase the event.

On a previous trip to the shop I purchased a beautiful silver meditation ring and I have rarely seen bracelets, earrings and necklaces as beautiful and affordable as what WIGG carries. Each piece is unique and the ladies who work in the store are happy to share the story about the provenance of each item they sell.

Downtown Cambridge is well worth allotting a whole day to browse the lovely shops. Treat yourself to a delicious lunch at the Cambridge Mill Restaurant overlooking The Grand River that runs through the middle of the old town of Galt, about forty minutes west of Toronto. And if you go on a Saturday, the amazing farmers' market is smack-dab across the road from the *WIGG* shop so you can load up on fresh Ontario fruit and veggies, cheeses, jams, honey and other local offerings. Go shopping girlfriend and support other women.

Chapter 7
Business

T-T-Takin' Care of Business
Bachman-Turner Overdrive, 1973

Sharing a little computer problem
in case it happens to you

Santa brought me a new laptop, replacing my ten-inch-screen HP with a seventeen-inch Toshiba. And changing computers never comes without a great deal of frustration, agony and an avalanche of R-rated bad-swears. After a month of fiddling, down-loading and tweaking I thought I finally had it nailed. Then, in early February, a pop-up indicated Toshiba had several new updates for me to download. Without hesitation, I clicked okay and thus began a month of catastrophes. The download took almost all day which should have been my first indication that something was not right. Then, when I re-booted, all my software including Microsoft Office, my toolbars and other packages had disappeared. Most of my old documents however were still intact. And there were several new so-called data savers and anti-virus packages listed in my program files.

After getting nowhere with Toshiba's on-line help I called their telephone customer service line which turned out to be equally inept. After nearly an hour of explaining and re-explaining my problem while the service rep kept repeating his scripted "I understand" and having me do the same series of keyboard exercises over and over, I finally gave up and hung up. Then I started the long, tedious process of having to reinstall everything and try to sort out the mess.

Several years ago, at the suggestion of a friend, I signed up for Carbonite backup system and it has proven its worth many times over. I wasn't confident that Carbonite was working on my new computer so I called them and got a really nice lady by the name of Elizabeth who was located in Maine—no off-shore English-as-a-second-language issues. She spoke to me like a real human being who wasn't reading from a script. She took over my computer and discovered several packages that were blocking the functioning of my proper virus software and Carbonite. She removed them, reinstalled my Carbonite and restored my files.

She mentioned that she had also recently purchased a Toshiba laptop and when I mentioned my experience with their update, she indicated she would get hers checked out with the people in her building who know more about computers than she does just to be on the safe side. I felt validated and vindicated.

The point of this story is if you have a new computer, particularly a Toshiba, be very, very careful about downloading their updates. What I had may have been a virus but I'll never know. All I know is that I'll never ever download anything from them again. And I'll certainly be extra diligent about other software updates coming my way. It's one of the few times; I wish I still had the services of my former employer's I.T. Department to help me out of these situations. Just one small downside of retirement!

Dear Mr. Gates and the rest of you bast@#$%

I try to keep up, I really do. But it's becoming increasingly more difficult for me to be our household I.T. Manager. Why can't the so-called brilliant minds at our high-tech companies devise gadgets that work like they should – the first time – and stay working. The problems of maintaining all our electronic gadgets is becoming too much for me to manage.

Yesterday, my husband spent more than an hour on the phone with a technician about a new password. Speaking of which, I have more than two full pages of passwords for accessing various sites and accounts – apparently all for my own safety. That means changing forgotten passwords regularly, which they say is a good idea but I'm not so sure. The only person who can't access my accounts is me. And my husband has only once in the last several years been able to successfully change the toner cartridge in his printer by himself without having a major meltdown.

About a year ago when I visited my eighty-eight-year old father I inadvertently did something with his TV remote control that was so catastrophic he felt it necessary to go out and replace the television. He now hides his controls whenever I visit to keep them out of my hands.

He only watches three channels. When I visited again recently, I noticed that despite paying for high-definition satellite and having a new high-def TV (see above) he was not getting Canadian networks in high-def. A rather protracted call to Shaw involved several service reps until I finally got one who spoke English as a first language and one whom I could hear (I'm hard-of-hearing). After more than an hour of performing various combinations of commands, I was informed we had to update the "thingie" in the satellite dish on the roof. With enormous trepidation we made the appointment for a technician to come out. And now my Dad's TV is screwed up again. I'm out of the will and he's never going to change channels again as long as he lives.

Electronic equipment's built-in obsolescence requires we replace our computers, receivers, phones and modems every couple of years. Just thinking about the horrors of that process causes me to break out in a cold sweat and make an appointment with a shrink for some serious drugs. A change in equipment never works right the first time without spending hours on technical issues. And then, things look different which requires a shift in mental approach. Windows Eight and Yahoo Mail's most recent upgrades nearly put me over the edge. I still haven't recovered.

Why can't all you high-tech companies simplify things so that ordinary people are not put through all this stress? It's jeopardizing my marriage, I'm probably cut out of my parents' will and it's making my hair fall out. And I can think of many things I'd sooner be doing with the five or six hours a day I spend trying to coerce your gadgets to cooperate. Fortunately I do not have a "Smart" phone or I would probably have been institutionalized by now. Instead I manage reasonably well with a thirteen dollars and fifty cents-per-month amplified cell phone I got through CARP (Canadian Association of Retired People) that allows me to do more than I care to know.

And for the privilege of experiencing all this stress and frustration I am paying in the neighbourhood of two hundred and fifty dollars a month which I'm thinking would be much better spent on wine.

Please hear my plea, Mr. Gates. It's all becoming too much.

P.S. And, no, I will not click on "Help". My nerves are just too fragile.

Dear Mr. Gates. It's me again – Lynda

I wrote you a while ago about the difficulties involved in keeping up with changing technology. While I love all the new advances we're making, it's getting harder and harder for me to cope. And I do not see why you cannot make things better.

Here's what I would like you to do. When I buy a new electronic gadget, I don't think I'm being unreasonable in asking that when I plug it in and fire it up, it recognizes all my previous data without me having to transfer, download, install new software and insert a thread of my DNA into the USB port. Maybe that's the answer. I'd even be willing to slice off a piece of my flesh and have the DNA validated, just so I wouldn't have to go through all the pain I experienced with getting my two new laptops to do what they should.

Santa kindly brought me and my honey new laptops for Christmas. Now that I'm blogging, my ten-inch screen just wasn't doing the job, so I wrote Santa and asked him for a new laptop with a seventeen-inch screen. And my guy was constantly whining about getting my hand-me-downs that always seemed second-best to him. You would think I'd have learned by now that such changes automatically come with hours of frustration, consuming reams of paper for recording new passwords and a tsunami of blue air. And you didn't disappoint.

I also recently signed up for a free trial month of NetFlix, not realizing the hours involved, again, in installing new software and reconfiguring my entire digital footprint just so I could watch a movie from my computer. It was suggested that I buy an inexpensive but effective little gadget called "Chromecast" which would eliminate the need for HDMI cables and lord knows what else. Sounded pretty simple! Needless to say, it *WASN'T*. I'm still working on that one. I did manage to watch one movie the other day but I don't remember what sequence of mouse clicks I employed and I'm not optimistic I can duplicate this achievement again. And I'm too scared to try.

Please Mr. Gates, when you introduce new products and software, make the transition easy. Is that asking too much? If you would design for *me* – probably your lowest common denominator – you would make millions of people happy. I can't take much more of this.

Your friend (but not for long),
Lynda

Hearing voices

Is it just me or does anyone else frequently find the female voices in media hard to listen to? Whatever happened to professional delivery, modulation and enunciation? While everyone can't sound like CBC's Shelagh Rogers, I think a few lessons at the Lorne Green School of Broadcasting for some would be of great benefit. Like many Boomers, I now wear teeny tiny expensive hearing aids and the little-girl nasally voices of so many women in media hurts my ears and annoys me to no end.

For example, Sirius satellite radio (siriuscanada.ca) once had a one-hour program on Canada Talks Channel 167 every afternoon called SpeakEasy hosted by Canadian Carla Collins who was actually in Los Angeles. Her voice is so easy to listen to. On the other hand, that program is preceded by "Ward and Al" and Al's voice drives me up the wall. Although I love the show and enjoy Allison's smart wit and intelligence it always sounds like she's yelling from across the room. Ouch! I have to turn the volume on the radio down. Allison, get closer to the microphone, lower the timbre a bit and stop yelling – please! Less treble, more bass.

The Marilyn Denis Show on CTV (marilyn.ca) often features Marilyn's stylist, Alexis Honce, who also needs voice modification. Her nasal, thin delivery grates on my nerves. There are many more women in media who were hired for skills other than voice but a bit of attention to this issue would sure be appreciated. These high-pitched little-girl voices are painful to listen to. After all, my voice is perfection, particularly my singing – just ask my husband. On the other hand, better not.

It's about those Honda Civics

Boomer Broads (Killer B's) may remember a song from the late fifties called "The Little Nash Rambler and the Cadillac". It describes the humiliation of the driver of an expensive, high-powered Cadillac whose ego is shattered when overtaken on the road by a little Nash Rambler, a fifties version of the Smart Car. In today's world it's Honda Civics that are overtaking us on the road and that's not a good thing.

It seems to me that every arsehole on the highway which is dangerously jumping lanes to gain precious inches or tailgating in speeding traffic is always driving a Honda Civic. In fact, I would go so far as to suggest that the driver is a sunglass-wearing male, in his twenties, with the driver's seat tilted back to an angle that makes even seeing the road a challenge, which I suppose helps disguise the fact they're texting while driving. And his car stereo can be heard clear from Toronto to Vancouver. Is there something in the Honda Civic owner's manual that stipulates that their vehicles must be driven at death-defying speeds or the warranty is voided? Are Civics that maneuverable and finely tuned that no other car can match its dexterity and nimbleness?

I genuinely try to be conscientious about obeying traffic rules. I'm considerate and yield when someone wants to get into my lane and I do not tailgate, unlike most men I know. I only drive in the outside passing lane when I'm actually passing and I do not hesitate to correct my friends when they fail to do the same. There's nothing more endearing than having a friend in the passenger seat to point out their driving infractions.

Those Honda Civic drivers, however, will be the death of me and I'm afraid, literally. When they misbehave on the road as they are wont to do, I want to drive my little old lady SUV right up their hatchbacks and park on their windshields until they feel the full weight of my wrath.

Perhaps the solution is to make it illegal to sell Honda Civics to anyone under the age of fifty. If Baby Boomers were the only eligible qualified buyers then I could cruise peacefully along Highway 401, 407 or QEW listening to my Bob Dylan anthology without fear of being bumper-car'd off the road. Or—I have an even better idea. Let's lobby Honda to market Civics to boomers exclusively and make them available in one colour only—Mary Kay pink. If they ran commercials with old ladies like me tooting off to our book club meetings and mani-pedi appointments driving a Honda Civic, perhaps they would lose their cool factor. After all, we are surely a demographic larger than the twenty-somethings. A spinoff benefit would be fewer thefts. Honda Civics are the most frequently stolen vehicle on the market. What self-respecting dude would want to steal or even be seen driving a pink car associated with old Boomer Broads. *Beep beep, beep beep*! Don't mess with Killer B's. *We're only in second gear.*

With this ring, I thee divorce

Whatever would I do without my morning *Globe and Mail* for inspiration? Today's issue concerns divorce. In the Business section, Bryan Borzykowski profiled a Montreal jeweler seeking advice on how to increase sales in a line of rings that celebrate the freedom associated with divorce. *Break-Up Gems* concluded that with forty percent of marriages ending in divorce there's a market for people wanting to have a tangible reminder of their new-found freedom.

Three marketing experts offered their advice. Axle Davids of Distillery Branding recommended the company focus more on the positive feelings associated with the divorced person's new status and the story behind it. Sandy Huang of Pinpoint Tactics takes this a step further and suggests also providing supportive information to people going through a divorce. Finally, Sanjay Singhal of Audiobooks.com recommends the jeweler research and purs more effective and accurate targeting of the specific market niche in search of such products.

Now, what you've been waiting for—my own take on this dilemma; as a retired corporate marketing professional and previously divorced Boomer, I can't resist offering my own opinion. First of all, I think the original assumption is misguided. Having a high divorce rate doesn't automatically translate into a potential marketing bonanza for this demographic. Divorce for most people is a painful, last-resort action that does not call for celebration. Grieving tends to be the more appropriate response. However, for those individuals who are thrilled to be "let out of jail free (or broke)," marking the event with a celebratory piece of jewelry is understandable.

Break-Up Gems' website is in the process of changing its name to freedomgems.com. That's a good start. Focus on the positive. In reviewing their website, I was not impressed with the selection of jewelry offered. In my opinion, most of it was not particularly unique and in no way enticed me to click on "Add to Cart". The prices were reasonable but the designs were as ordinary as something I could pick up from impulse purchases beside the cash register at any gift or card shop across the country.

If I'm going to purchase a piece of jewelry I want it to be unusual, a conversation piece, and unlike anything else I have. It must make a statement and if it involves recycled precious metals and stones, that's even better. For example, last year I purchased on-line a stainless steel bangle made from parts of guns turned in during an amnesty in Newark, New Jersey. The bracelet has a hammered finish and is inscribed with the serial number of the gun from which it was made. That's different. I wear it every day and delight in telling people the story behind it.

Mr. Pinkesz, I suggest you go back to the drawing board and come up with some really kick-ass designs. Take Sanjay Singhal's advice and re-evaluate your marketing strategy to target this very specific niche. Ignore Sandy Huang's suggestion to broaden the offering to include supportive information. Stick to your core business—making jewelry, and don't pretend to be a shrink. There are definitely people out there who want this kind of thing but you'll never get rich on it. Go with the advice behind door number three, Mr. Sanjay Singhal—and of course my own brilliant suggestions.

Tipping my hard hat to one of the best

Today I would like to pay tribute to my old alma mater, EllisDon Corporation. Geoff Smith, President of ED was in Monaco (yes, the real one, next to Italy) last week representing Canada's nomination for International Entrepreneur of the Year, in a prestigious award ceremony hosted annually by Ernst & Young. That's serious recognition and one EllisDon can be justifiably proud of.

When I joined the firm in 1971, I'd never even heard of the company. At that time they completed sixty-five million dollars in new construction each year and there were only slightly more than fifty people at our Toronto Christmas party. They now complete in the neighbourhood of four *billion* dollars annually and their Christmas parties are attended by more people than a Stones' concert. In more than thirty years at EllisDon I had the privilege of working with both the founder Don Smith and later, one of his sons, Geoff Smith. The corporate culture originally established by Don Smith and further advanced by Geoff does not follow typical business school models yet it resulted in a highly successful, uniquely-styled company that for the past several years has consistently been recognized as one of Canada's top employers and best-managed companies.

The recipe is not that complicated but it is unusual in the business world. EllisDon is not stricturted by hierarcial protocols, formal policies and corporate dogma. The management structure is relatively flat and employees are strongly encouraged to put their ideas forward. If it's a good idea and it flies, great. If not—it was a lesson learned, deal with the consequences and carry on. Senior managers are accessible, open and supportive of innovation. I doubt I could have done as well as I did in another type of organization and ED employees who can take the heat thrive in this type of environment.

My husband, George and I both have deep and strong roots at EllisDon. George also spent most of his career at EllisDon and for many years was number two guy under Don Smith and then Geoff. We're both so proud of our small part in helping create this incredible company. I follow EllisDon's website and read Geoff's blogs regularly just so I can retain that feeling of being part of a very special family that has matured and keeps getting better in ways I could never have imagined. As Geoff so often and readily states, it's a combined effort by a group of incredibly bright, hard-working, creative and talented men and women. This international recognition confirms it.

The solution for Canadian retailers is as easy as 1, 2, 3

Here I am back on my soapbox because Canadian retailers do not seem to be listening to me – at their peril. Their strange, blinkered attitude toward the customer is responsible for so many of their problems and they seem oblivious. The solution is as easy as one, two, and three. Let me give you a few recent examples that demonstrate my point.

Yesterday I went into Tiffany's in Yorkdale Mall in Toronto. I knew exactly what I wanted to see – a necklace that comes in three sizes and I wanted to compare the sizes and prices to determine what my husband is getting me for Christmas. I'm an informed shopper.

I was met by a "greeter" like in a car dealership. That alone annoyed me because she couldn't help me and had to go and interrupt two chatting sales associates to get one to come and assist me. Unnecessary delay number one: The sales associate came over and I pointed out the silver necklaces in the display case, however, none of the sizes on display were what I wanted. I had to tell him there was a larger size available which required him to go to the computer to verify my information. Unnecessary delay number two: Then he had to dig in a locked drawer for it. Finally, he unwrapped the medium and large sizes. I indicated that ideally I would like the medium size but with the longer chain that comes with the large size. No comment from the sales person. So I asked the question, "Can I get the medium size with the longer chain?" Then he volunteered that I could but at an extra cost per inch of silver chain. Why did he not tell me this helpful information when I was comparing the two, to satisfy my requirement and clinch the sale? Phew! It seemed like a lot of work on my part – the customer – to inform the sales person. Which brings me to my first suggestion for retailers?

1. Share product knowledge with customer. If you don't have this knowledge, it's your job to get it. Oh, and ditch the greeters. What's the point?

During a visit to J. Crew & Co. I spotted some gorgeous faux pearls on a mannequin. The string of pearls was extremely long and looped very fashionably over a denim shirt. I asked a sales person to show me the long string of pearls. She couldn't find them. Looked everywhere but the washroom; finally, I brought to her attention that it looked like the display was actually two strings of pearls clipped together for that particular look. Again, why did I have to provide the product knowledge? Not only could she not find the short string of pearls, but she couldn't see that it was actually two sets linked together.

2. Know your inventory and where it is. Again, this is not the job of the customer.

And thanks to Hudson's Bay's chronic and severe lack of sales staff, I nearly witnessed a riot in the women's section of the Mississauga Square One store during "Bay Day" sales. There are only three cash desks in the very busy women's department of a very busy store. I spotted some jeans on sale but not in my size. Naturally there are no sales associates walking the floor to assist me, so I hiked across the floor and lined up with eight others to ask a cashier. When I finally worked my way to the second position in the line, the woman in front of me had a customer service issue that required calling a manager and debating store policy in great detail. Meanwhile the rest of us in line were waiting, fuming.

Finally a second clerk appeared who was slower than I ever thought possible at processing sales. I got her. Naturally she informed me that "if the size I wanted isn't out, then they don't have it." I had waited fifteen minutes for that bit of obvious information. So I asked her to check the computer to see if perhaps they did in fact have my size buried somewhere else in the store. More minutes passed and no, they did not. So, then I asked if they had them in another store and could they get them for me. Fully another twenty minutes passed while at my insistence she searched, found the jeans and processed the sale. Hallelujah. By now, the women behind me were forming a lynch mob. Many were on their lunch hour and simply left. I actually felt sorry for the sales ladies who were hopelessly overworked and understaffed.

3. Can retailers not scratch up a few pennies to hire adequate sales people to actually work the floor and help customers? Maybe add a few extra cash registers while you're at it. Eliminating a couple of pairs of jeans would raise the money needed to pay them.

My experiences shopping in the United States, the U.K. and Europe have been very different and positive. Sales associates are well-trained, genuinely helpful, capable of actually thinking and are wonderfully plentiful. It's not that complicated. I guarantee if Canadian retailers would listen to me they'd see sales increase. Isn't that what they're in business for? And with Christmas coming, it's only going to get worse. Now that I've vented, I feel a bit better, but not much.

Retail rant hits home

My recent rant about the poor level of service in the retail sector really touched a nerve with my readers. We all have horror stories to relate and retailers just don't seem to be listening. I've been writing Hudson's Bay for years about their frustrating shortage of sales personnel without any acknowledgement of my concerns. Once I even typed a nice letter on real vellum paper, hand-inked my signature at the bottom and mailed it with an actual old-fashioned stamp to the President of Hudson's Bay at 401 Bay Street in Toronto. I naively thought the novelty of a personal letter delivered by a human mail carrier might get his attention, but no response. Maybe a Strip-O-Gram would have been a better idea – more nineteenth century.

That changed this week however. I e-mailed the Manager of Square One's Hudson's Bay store with a link to my blog posting and received a response within two hours. The e-mail was personal, acknowledging and agreeing with my comments. He further described changes he has already made and assured me there are more coming. Holy smokers! I nearly fell off my old-lady easy chair. I also e-mailed Tiffany's but no response so far. Guess I'll have to take my millions of shopping dollars elsewhere. They'll be sorry.

Sometimes I feel like the cartoon character grouchy old Maxine with her little dog at her feet. I've worked hard all my life and always gave more than asked for in every job I did. All I expect from others is delivery of basic job requirements and that's not unreasonable.

Since many Boomer Broads are now retired we are in a position (time-wise) to make ourselves heard. The next time you receive poor service or an indifferent attitude, speak up or get your gnarly arthritic old fingers doing the walking across your keyboard. Collectively we can make a difference. And I don't want to hear it's not your job. I can't do this on my own.

I did it. You're welcome

Today as I was standing in the supermarket-style lineup to check out at the Hudson's Bay store in Square One in Mississauga, I heard an announcement that nearly knocked me on saggy old fanny. "Attention shoppers. If you cannot find the size you need in our store, we will search other Hudson's Bay locations and have it sent to your home" or words to that effect. I'm convinced this small step toward customer service is entirely a result of my blog in November gently advising the retail industry how they could improve business, followed by my Retail Rant Hits Home blog. After all, I'm also convinced that millions read my blog and take action when required. The store manager actually responded to my e-mail at the time which impressed this old broad to no end.

One tiny glitch in today's transaction (which is a fairly significant one) is that the cashier failed to give me my Bay Day twenty-five percent discount on the clearly marked sale price and charged me full price for both items. My bringing it to her attention—despite the fact the store is emblazoned with red and white banners and sale signs—reduced my final bill by fifty percent.

We're making progress Boomer Broads, one small step at a time. Perhaps someday Hudson's Bay stores will have enough staff that the sales associate will have the time to walk around the counter, hand me my bag, smile and say thank you. Let's just say, I too have a dream.

All we need is love

The Baby Boomers are a demographic bulge that is hard to ignore – at least you would think so. Until you become a fifty-plus Baby Boomer. That's when advertisers and marketers get stupid about the huge impact of our spending power as they continue to focus on the eighteen to forty-five age group. If we're not ignored completely, as in fashion and clothing, we are represented as incontinent codgers blissfully swing-dancing at the seniors' club or as love-struck empty nesters dropping everything to run and take advantage of our partner's four-hour erection.

I read recently that the average age for creative types at ad agencies is twenty-eight. Even with the supervision of a more mature ad executive perhaps in their thirties or forties, they're still not "getting us." Print ads and TV commercials continue to portray Boomers as a throwback to earlier generations in need of a variety of pharmaceuticals to get us through the day or night. Some Boomers may have embraced the early drug culture but that doesn't mean we aim to become geriatric junkies. Depends™ are not what Kris Kristofferson had in mind when he sang "Help Me Make It through the Night."

What is it going to take for marketers to wake up to what we're about? It's really not that complicated. We're a generation who have been interested and involved in politics since we were old enough to vote, which cannot be said of most generations who followed. We marched and in some cases were killed (Kent State) to make our concerns heard. Our anti-war beliefs were backed up by our welcoming and support of Vietnam draft-dodgers who came to Canada. We wore peace symbols, lived The Beatles' "All You Need Is Love" anthem and pushed for changes in how society treats women, gays and lesbians and minorities. In fact, as I watched The Night That Changed America, a live tribute to fiftieth anniversary of The Beatles' appearance on Ed Sullivan, my eyes teared up as I watched Paul lead everyone in singing All You Need Is Love in a déjà vu moment with Ringo drumming in the background. Fifty years have flown by but Paul and Ringo, looking fit and hip *get it*.

While we no longer wear love beads, peace symbols and flowered shirts with our bell bottoms, we still have a huge interest in how we look, how we dress and how this world performs. The current portrayal of our retiring generation as one who needs nothing more than an assortment of prescription meds, incontinence products, stair chairs and denture adhesives is insulting, myopic and certainly not accurate.

Wouldn't it be wonderful to see attractive sixty-somethings strolling down the fashion runways in avante-guarde flattering designs that do not involve embroidered teddy bears and strawberries around the neckline? To be able to buy sexy, comfortable nightgowns or PJs that don't look like dorm-wear or at the other end of the spectrum, brothel-wear would be a joy. Would someone please design casual clothing that could confidently turn heads on the streets of Paris or New York for Boomers who are not size zero? We are still cool. We still have our own teeth, albeit perhaps enhanced with expensive veneers, we're physically fit and we're smart, informed and involved.

Boomers are not all interested in altering our faces with plastic surgery, Botox or fillers until we resemble freaks. We respect Boomers like Diane Keaton, Helen Mirren and Meryl Streep who aren't afraid to show their earned age. We don't want sugared cereals – in fact we'd love to eliminate sugar from most of our foods. We want to eat healthy non-GMO'd food. We want stylish clothes that fit and are flattering. We want bungalows with two car-garages, large closets and open-plan living space close to urban centres so we can go to the theatre (both live and movie) and have plenty of shopping options. We want to be able to remain in the tech loop without jumping on every new gadget that hits the market. We're educated, curious and still growing intellectually. The cup is only half full and we intend to keep filling it until it overflows, then we'll order another cup on Amazon. And we do have a sense of humour about our place in the scheme of things.

The world of consumer marketing is the ultimate loser here. We have the need, the want and the financial wherewithal to get this country back on track but it seems no one is listening. Even our new-found advocate groups like CARP and AARP struggle to be heard. Perhaps it's time we once again strapped on the old love beads, boarded buses and banged on the doors of government, retailers, advertisers and businesses to get their attention.

In the meantime, make your voice heard however you can – by e-mail, phone calls to appropriate parties or boycott institutions that will not listen to what we have to say. If I see another ad on TV for meds I don't need or that represent a lifestyle that does not respect who we really are, I might have to let out my bell bottoms and start marching. In the meantime, I'm trying my best with blogging, e-mails and personal advocacy. There's plenty of room left in my cup. How about yours?

Hello Saks, Goodbye Bay

They did it again. Another national retailer has made a major decision without consulting me first. Hudson's Bay Company has decided to relinquish their flagship Queen Street store in Toronto to their newly-acquired Saks. I would have thought that after Cadillac Fairview's weird decision to put a Florida-style drive-through retail "mall" at Don Mills Road and Lawrence Avenue they would have learned their lesson. When

Don Mills Centre opened a couple of years ago, I thoughtfully wrote Cadillac Fairview Corporation to inform them of their folly and suggested they consult me on all future major decisions. I'm a shopping pro and have a life-time of expert on-the-job experience. Every time I go Don Mills Centre (twice to be precise) it's been raining and I've had to dodge raindrops to get from store to store. And the stores, other than McEwen's Foods are the same ubiquitous, boring mall haunts available a couple of miles up the road at Fairview Mall. At least Fairview is enclosed and has a subway stop. I've never ventured to Don Mills Centre in winter so I've been spared climbing snowbanks and stomping salty slush off my boots when I enter a store.

Now they've gone and done it again. But this time, I actually see the value in their strategy. The Hudson's Bay Company has been throwing millions of dollars at refurbishing their Queen Street store at the expense of their Bloor and Yonge location which is tired, poorly organized and just plain cranky. My first reaction was surprise because of the above-mentioned investment in Queen Street (does anyone remember the Creed's fiasco?). Then I thought – a Saks location on Bloor Street just one block away from major competitor Holt-Renfrew is just plain vulgar. The Queen Street location is handier to Bay Street office towers and all those insider-trading dollars and service-charge wealthy bankers, not to mention all the tourists who come to Toronto for the one thousand dollars per seat Leafs' games. They can just take the "PATH" to Saks on Queen Street without getting salt stains on their Manolo Blanik's.

But this is all rather anti-climactic compared to Nordstrom, my most favourite shopping destination coming to town. In only two years I'll have my very own Nordstrom store at Sherway Gardens in Etobicoke. I understand they're also locating in Yorkdale but that place is such a zoo I avoid it like carbs after Christmas. If the parking constraints at Yorkdale and the constant crush of shopping bodies don't get you, the traffic on adjoining Highway 401 when you're trying to escape will. Nordstrom is not quite as high-end as Saks and they have a more interesting mix of merchandise than Hudson's Bay Company, with better store layouts. And they actually carry great fashions not designed for prepubescent anorexics. One of my major complaints with Hudson's Bay (which I've also considerately written to the President of the company about) is their lack of sales personnel to assist shoppers. Nordstrom has friendly staff in adequate numbers to service us promptly and considerately. Instead of having an over-worked snarky sales clerk toss a plastic bag across the counter at you in a Hudson's Bay store, the Nordstrom sales associates kindly walk around the counter and personally place a lovely silver Nordstrom shopping bag in your eager little hand. And if they don't have the size or colour you want, *they actually offer to source it at another store and have it delivered to your home*, free of charge if you have an account! Holy smokes! No wonder I love them. And their ladies' washrooms are far superior to those at Hudson's Bay Company, but then everyone's are better than the Hudson's Bay loo's.

Shopping is a life skill I've acquired through a lot of hard work and years of dedication. I love strolling through a store, touching and feeling the merchandise, casting judgments on its fashionability and quality and rejoicing when I score a major bargain. My Boomer Broad friends and I have a finely-tuned system for retail reconnaissance. Shopping with a buddy is verboten – a waste of time and talent. We split up, spread out and we each pursue our own shopping agenda. Then we meet for lunch over a glass of wine; have a preview show and tell, then disperse for more shopping. We spend the first few hours visually scoping things out, then at the end of the day after reviewing all that we've seen, return to the stores and items we've decided to purchase just before we leave. That minimizes mistakes and returns.

I'll forgive Hudson's Bay for not consulting me this time but if they don't start listening to my advice, they're headed for trouble. My Boomer Broad posse and I are a pretty significant demographic and because we're at an age where our estrogen tanks are a bit low, we have the ability to bring down entire market sectors. Just look at what happened to "New Coke." If retailers continue to ignore us – well, let's just say we warned you.

Take my advice and live happily ever after

If I had my life to do over, there are many things I would do differently, both in business and personally. Not a whole lot, as my mistakes and wrong turns are part of what makes me the fabulous person I am today. But with some tweaking, life could have been an easier, more satisfying journey. So, I'm now going to dish out some advice, primarily for young women who will be retired someday and will hopefully make better decisions than I did when I was young.

About fifteen years ago, I read a book published in 1992 called *Your Money or Your Life* by Joe Dominguez and Vicki Robin and that book changed my perspective on life. The book had been recommended in a sermon by a United Church minister who entered the ministry after a career in the business world. He had his MBA as well as other degrees and I figured he should know what he was talking about.

The strong message that came through in this book is the importance of financial independence. **The book suggested that the sooner we are financially independent the sooner we can do what really satisfies us in life.** This is not a selfish undertaking. It's a simple survival skill. You cannot become a philanthropist, a full-time volunteer, an artist or whatever else you would rather be doing with your life until you have the resources behind you to support the lifestyle.

The phrase that most resonated with me was "sell yourself to the highest bidder in the short-term for long-term gain." In a perfect world we would all have jobs or careers that we love so much it's not work, but this is realistically not going to be the case for most of us.

At the time I read this book, during the recession of the 1990s, I was self-employed and a long way from financial independence. I was also in my fifties so time was running out. That's when I made the decision to go back into the corporate world where I would have a regular pay cheque and I could start putting my financial house in order. Which brings me to my first piece of advice:

Sock away as much money as possible from an early age. The reason for this is so that by the time you reach your fifties you will have options. When you reach your fifties, your view of life and your priorities may be very different from what you wanted in your twenties. You may no longer have the energy or enthusiasm for your career/job that you once did and if you have a sizeable nest-egg you will be able to make lifestyle adjustments to accommodate new wants and needs. Without this financial independence you're a slave to the master indefinitely. And you will not remember purchasing those designer shoes that seemed so important twenty years earlier and set you back a week's pay.

I'm not about to tell you how to manage your money but be very wary of any kind of debt. This means not using credit unless absolutely necessary and only for large purchases such as a house or car. Many young people are so crippled by consumer debt arising from living beyond their means that they will never get their heads above water. Pay your credit card balances off every month and contribute to retirement savings plans and other safe investment vehicles every year without fail.

So, do whatever you can make the most money and still be reasonably happy while you are young. Save as much as you can. The cumulative effects of saving even ten dollars per week add up with compound interest.

Do not risk ruining yourself financially for material goods. You can look good, feel good and be good without running up crippling consumer debt. If being a bridesmaid at a destination wedding is a financial hardship for you, decline the invitation. It'll be the bride's loss and your gain. If you can't afford a new car, drive a reliable "previously owned" vehicle that meets your needs instead of your wants or take advantage of public transit.

I didn't think about retirement saving until I was in my forties. While it's never too late, if I'd started in my twenties and accounting for compound interest, I could have accumulated a sizeable nest egg much earlier and not had to worry about money in mid-life. Unfortunately, when we're in our twenties and even thirties, we seem to need a lot of money for education, houses, cars, kids, vacations and all the other demands of daily life.

It really is as simple as **"pay yourself first"**. Just as surely as your rent or mortgage payment comes out of your bank account on a certain day each month, set up a plan to save the same way. There are hundreds of excellent books available to help you plan your spending and saving. Whether you use the jar system, payroll deductions or online tracking apps, plenty of help is at your fingertips. Banks will automatically transfer money from your account into savings and investments. As Nike so eloquently puts it, "Just do it". You'll never miss the money and I guarantee you'll have a more satisfied middle and old age when you're financially secure. And you'll have a cushion in the case of an emergency such as losing your job while you are young.

Protect your interests and take care of yourself first. We're all familiar with the airline safety procedure telling us to put the oxygen mask over our own face before that of children. The benefits may seem obvious to most of us but not everyone gets it. This metaphor applies to life in general and in my experience no more so than in the business world.

Boomer Broads were raised to be dutiful, considerate, self-effacing models of compliance. In a generation of women who were now expected to also hold our own in the working world, we carried these values into the workplace. As a result, we were easily taken advantage of and not always given our just rewards. How many Boomers and other women do you know who worked their asses off and never received the recognition they deserved.

I remember the days when Help Wanted ads in the newspaper were worded, **Help Wanted – Male**, and **Help Wanted – Female**. In the early 1970s, a friend of mine was an early challenger of the implicit disadvantages for women in this system. Jeannette worked on the order desk for an international chemical company, a job shared with one other person, a man. Jeannette made ninety-six dollars per week and the man sitting beside her made one hundred and seventeen dollars per week to do exactly the same work. When he gave notice he was leaving the company, they advertised in the Help Wanted – Male section of the paper and offered a salary of one hundred and seventeen dollars per week. Jeannette applied for the job and set in motion turmoil at her company that left her wondering whether she would even retain the job she had. Her employers were unaccustomed to such a challenge, but Jeannette figured she could use the extra twenty-one dollars per week and she was doing the job already. After a great deal of huffing and puffing on the part of her employer, she was awarded the matching salary.

That was the beginning of changing times. While Jeannette's situation seems unbelievable by today's standards where equality is assumed, it was somewhat radical at the time. There are still subtle forms of discrimination in the workplace today but for the most part, we've made progress.

One area I think where some women still struggle is in being assertive in stating and insisting upon rewards we have earned. A few years after my friend's experience, I too felt I was being underpaid for the work I was performing so I decided some action was required. I read one of the early books on corporate gamesmanship for women called *Games Mother Never Taught You* by Betty Lehan Harrigan and set about doing my homework. I researched other businesses to see what my work was worth on the market. I summarized my strengths and weaknesses, my contributions to the corporate bottom line and overall corporate business practices. I made a list of anticipated questions and objections I might face and developed strong, appropriate responses. I detailed exactly what I wanted and why I felt I deserved it. I outlined a future plan for my job. I even had girlfriends quiz me and rehearse me so I'd be prepared.

The day of the interview I felt ready although somewhat nervous. When I walked into the room to face the Vice-President, I encountered not one but three Vice-Presidents, all sitting with smiles on their faces ready to take me on. I can even remember what I was wearing that day in 1980. It was a pink windowpane wool blazer with a black skirt and silk shirt with the requisite eighties matching silk bow tie. I was "dressed for success", although in retrospect a red blazer would have been a better choice. My heart starting pounding so hard, I looked down and could actually see my pearls vibrating on my silk shirt. I took a seat and launched into my well-rehearsed presentation. Fortunately, the interview went in my favour and I was awarded what I was asking for.

The point of this experience is that had I not taken the initiative, I would probably have never received what I deserved. That was more than thirty years ago and I didn't entirely learn my lesson. As the years went on, I continued to be a model of dedication and hard work but in retrospect, **I was never as assertive as I should or could have been**. When a female friend in a similar job at a competitor's firm left to accept a position doing the same work at another company for *twice* the salary, I congratulated her and carried on as before, working long hours and trying to "do it all".

What I learned is that it's the responsibility of each one of us when we are doing an excellent job to insist upon the commensurate rewards. That may take the form of a higher salary, a promotion, an extra week of vacation or some other type of recognition. I worked for a very enlightened employer who would probably have complied if I had raised the issue of higher salary or more staff. The fault was my own. Instead of asking for additional staff, my way of coping was to string yellow "CAUTION" tape up around my desk and work until midnight.

Take care of *yourself* in business. We've watched men to do it without hesitation. If I'd taken better care of myself, I'd have had more job satisfaction, a fatter pension and much lower cortisol levels. Do not be the dutiful, hardworking girl waiting for a pat on the head. Set your goals. State what you want and if you deserve it, ask for it. The worst they can say is no. At best, you'll be able to buy a condo and take a vacation. You're worth it. And buying your own diamonds proves it.

Dress for the job you want, not the one you already have. This advice is for those who have career ambitions. If you're happy with the status quo, that's okay too. Sometimes, life's more important events just get in the way or perhaps a career is not one of your priorities. For those who have set their sights on moving up in the workplace, I have a few words of advice related to **personal presentation**.

This may sound like a cliché you've heard before, but it is still valid. I once had lunch with a middle manager friend on a casual Friday. She was wearing blue jeans, sneakers and a gray hoodie. As we were discussing workplace issues, I found myself questioning her presentation and finally said, "How can you expect to be taken seriously as a manager when you're dressed like a university student?"

Depending on your corporate culture, casual Fridays have now grown in some workplaces to include the entire work week. But that does not mean you should ever be anything less than professional. While we no longer have to deck ourselves out in the "Dress For Success" plain suits and silk bow ties, there is still a standard to be observed. Showing too much skin or dressing provocatively is distracting and sends a message that you should be noticed for your sex appeal rather than your professional ability. There's plenty of help out there in the form of books, websites, personal consultants and even retail sales personnel if you need a bit of guidance.

Personal presentation also includes manners. Working at a construction company, I saw many managers and supervisors in the field with poor basic manners at business luncheons and other corporate functions, so I organized a day-long business etiquette seminar for anyone who wanted to attend. Some approached the issue with a casual level of disdain while others welcomed the opportunity to improve themselves. The facilitator covered everything from the proper use of fish forks (most attendees had never even seen a fish fork before), to how to dress, body language, entertaining for business, whether to order a drink before your guests arrive or even whether to order a drink at all. It was a very successful day and equipped a lot of people with the confidence they needed to conduct themselves properly at business functions.

Present yourself positively and excel at speaking in public. To some people, this is easy but for most of us it requires time and training to build the necessary skill set. I cannot say enough good things about Toastmasters International. I spent a winter attending their once-a-week evening sessions learning the basics of public speaking. Toastmasters builds skills by degrees, beginning with simple exercises such as delivering one-minute impromptu speeches from unknown "Table Topics" to more advanced presentations. I found their meetings incredibly helpful in building confidence by practising speaking in a supportive and encouraging environment. Watching my fellow Toastmasters members, commenting on their strengths and having them do the same for me was unbelievably helpful. I guarantee this will turn a dread of speaking in front of people into something to look forward to and actually enjoy. Thanks to Toastmasters, I progressed from being unable to even speak up at a meeting to making a presentation about corporate marketing that captured the front page of *The Globe and Mail's* business section. Never underestimate the impression you make on others – in the way you dress, the way you conduct yourself at corporate events and your ability to project a positive image. After all, you are a representative of your company and you should always put your best foot forward.

Breaking up is hard to do

Bette Davis is famously quoted as once saying, "Getting old is not for sissies." Retirement is a natural by-product of getting old. For some, it's wonderful; for others, not so much. I definitely fall into the former category but for those who are forced to retire before they're psychologically or financially ready it can be devastating.

At the risk of generalizing, I think it's often more difficult for men than women to retire. The Boomer generation and our parents' generation is rife with men who devoted their entire adult lives to their work. Perhaps it was a family business, a demanding business like medicine or maybe it was a prestigious corporate position. Then, when they retire they have lost not only something to do every day but their very identity.

When you're retired, people are no longer impressed by what you once did for a living. When you're not Mr. Big, President of ABC International Corporation it can create a huge vacuum. Because you no longer have the power to improve your former associates' lives they drop you from their social and business circle. This alienation is very difficult.

My friend David worked in the marketing department of a giant international corporation. The corporate culture was casual and creative with frequent product launches, brainstorming sessions, corporate retreats and big-budget product promotions. Co-workers often socialized outside of work hours going on skiing weekends and attending parties together. When David retired he expected his former coworkers to keep him in the loop but the invitations stopped. He was understandably confused and hurt that people he had always considered friends as well as co-workers no longer wanted his company.

Another executive I know from the financial services sector was similarly affected when suddenly dropped by his circle of business friends when he retired. He felt abandoned and couldn't understand why his calls weren't returned and no one wanted to join him for lunch anymore. Once the unspoken message became clear, he was forced to accept the truth – he was no longer a somebody. It turned out his business friends were in fact not real friends at all but purely business associates and when he could no longer do anything for them they no longer needed or wanted his company.

This particular aspect of retirement can result in feelings similar to divorce. That entity that has been a huge part of your life is gone and no longer cares to associate with you. I've experienced divorce and the sense of loss that goes with it – the loss of being part of a couple, loss of some friends, loss of half the house and assets. A new strategy for moving on is required. For some individuals it might take the form of part-time consulting work to keep a hand in the business world, albeit to a lesser degree. Others may prefer a more relaxed approach such as taking time to enjoy all the activities that working did not allow for. This can include golfing, taking courses, spending time with the grandkids, pursuing hobbies or perhaps a part-time job.

Retiring for me, however, meant total and utter freedom at last. Now I have the time to read voraciously, entertain at my leisure, get together with friends, take vacations whenever I please and do dozens of other things I've waited for my entire life. Fortunately, it was and is the best time of my life and just keeps getting better.

Over the years I have observed people in my work environment approaching retirement with different attitudes. Some were looking forward to having the time to travel and do things with friends. Others were bewildered and had no constructive plan for filling their time. Those who were not prepared were often the ones who developed health issues that may have contributed to an early demise. Interestingly, many of the retiring career women I have worked with were often the ones who had a Mediterranean cruise or a tour of Ireland scheduled for the week after they finished work. They had plans to volunteer at a library or hospital and hit the ground running. These are generally the people who live the longest and have the richest retirement.

Enjoying retirement does not have to involve memberships in expensive golf clubs or Mediterranean cruises. The simplest things can provide enormous pleasure. There's nothing better than enjoying a second cup of tea as I take my time over the morning paper. The luxury of being able to go grocery shopping minus the crowds on a Tuesday morning or hanging sheets outside on the line to dry in the morning breezes still makes me happy. The novelty of enjoying a ladies lunch with a chilled glass of Pino Grigio and not having to rush back to the office has still not worn off. Entertaining friends is much more pleasurable when you have the luxury of time to shop, cook and prepare for your guests.

Just like in a divorce situation, breaking up with your employer can be devastating or it can be your "get out of jail free" card. The outcome is entirely up to you but have a plan and be flexible. Crank up the sixties music and let's rock n' roll. As Boomer Broads we're living our best years now.

Succeeding where I failed

This morning's Globe and Mail contained a supplement from a gift basket company appropriately called "Baskits." Reading through the brochure took me back about twenty-five years when I was Corporate Marketing Manager for EllisDon Corporation and we were one of their first customers. Ann Kerrigan came into our office promoting her fledgling business at a time when we were looking to give our corporate clients a unique seasonal gift other than liquor or wine. At the time, gift baskets were a relatively new concept. Ann customized a folk-art wooden Canada goose stuffed with various nibblies and seasonal treats that totally wowed us with its originality. The next year, she sourced wooden toolboxes for us that included an assortment of small chocolate tools. How appropriate for a construction company.

Over the years we used Baskits for various corporate gift-giving requirements. Inevitably the competition grew and finding novel gifts became more challenging. But Ann and her partner Carla at Baskits held their own in a difficult market. And now they've been in business for more than twenty-five years. They're obviously doing something right – in fact a lot of things right. From a small cottage industry that began in Ann's apartment to a major business, Baskits has succeeded where so many others have not.

Creating gift baskets looks so easy. How complicated can it be to stash some yummies into a basket of shred? Wrap it in cello with a nice bow and you're all set. I once spent a day in Ann and Carla's warehouse just before Christmas when things are particularly hairy. Thought I'd help out but instead I was more of a liability. I burned holes in the shrink-wrap with the hair-dryer thingie, dropped a small bottle of sticky maple syrup on floor and broke it, struggled with the arrangements – and, you name it, I screwed it up. Understandably over time I would have improved and perhaps could even have become as skilled as Maria from El Salvador who worked there full-time. And the physical demands of being on your feet all day in front of huge tables, collecting goodies from warehouse shelves is no easy feat. And that's just the "creative" side" which Ann manages so artfully. Carla handles the complex business side of the operation.

Tipping my hat to Baskits. Well done, Ann and Carla.

Is an expensive education worth the investment?

A couple of weeks ago I attended a seminar for aspiring writers at Spadina Library in downtown Toronto. The guest speaker was Dr. Donna Kakonge, author of sixty-six books, a degree in journalism from Carleton University, a Master's Degree from Concordia University, the University of London International Programmes Bachelor of Laws, an All But "approved" Dissertation (ABD) with the OISE | University of Toronto in Curriculum, Teaching and Learning Development.

One of the other audience members, a teacher with a Master's Degree asked if it was recommended that she obtain additional education in order to further her writing ambitions. Kakonge was particularly well-qualified to answer the question and her definitive answer was "no".

We later had an interesting discussion about the payback for the cost of education. Kakonge's personal experience is particularly relevant because she is far more educated that most people and recognizes the veiled marketing strategies employed by educational institutions to sell their product. Education definitely has value but it is also a business that needs to feed and sustain itself. The past several decades have seen a remarkable growth in the level of education achieved by young people as well as working adults seeking to enhance their credentials.

Financial advisor Suze Orman consistently discourages people from dipping into their retirement fund or borrowing money to finance their children's education suggesting students take more responsibility for the cost. I agree with Kakonge that there comes a point where further education will not guarantee a better job. There are even employers who regard too much education as being out of touch with the realities of the business world. While this may not be the case when working in academia, it should be considered before borrowing tens of thousands of dollars for further education.

In his latest book, David & Goliath, Malcolm Gladwell takes this a step further and suggests that expensive Ivy League universities such as Harvard and Yale are possibly not worth the investment. Students who were top achievers in their local schools may become discouraged to find they are no longer top of their class in a prestige university teaching the crème de la crème. An excellent education can be achieved at a less expensive university.

As someone who often hired graduates when I was still working, I would often rely on street smarts and interpersonal skills ahead of high marks in the hiring process. In fact, college graduates often had a better grasp of the working world than university graduates and frequently were the better choice. The bottom line is education alone is not the sole determinant in the success of the individual in the working world. Practical learning really begins on the job and personal skills and aptitudes are extremely important. Do the simple math and make your decision about whether to get that big student loan based on sound judgment about your return on investment. Education is also a business that needs financial input. If you can afford it and like the work, then go for it.

On the other hand, do not let insufficient financial backing or lack of interest in education leave you feeling like a non-achiever. Some very successful people never finished college or university. Bill Gates, Steve Jobs, Peter Mansbridge, Rick Mercer and Diane Francis are examples of people who succeeded on their own merits. They worked hard and over the years built up their experience and credentials to achieve truly admirable levels of success in their fields.

When I retired I was Marketing Manager for an international corporation with annual sales in excess of two billion dollars, a job that theoretically should have been held by someone with a minimum of a marketing degree and probably an MBA. I completed high school, took a few evening college and university courses and business seminars and created my own career by doing a variety of crappy jobs until I got into something I enjoyed doing, had an aptitude for and was given the chance by a very liberal employer to run with it.

I'm a huge believer in learning on the job but you have to start somewhere and that's never at or anywhere near the top. You have to earn your stripes by doing all kinds of less-than-desirable jobs to learn the basics such as showing up on time, doing your best regardless of the task, exceeding expectations, and learning about money management, deadlines and other basic job requirements.

Being too focused on one career goal from a young age can often result in young people not taking advantage of unplanned-for tangential employment opportunities that could grow into something wonderful. Engineers, lawyers and Chartered Accountants for example have the advantage of being marketable in professions other than their professional designation. When we Baby Boomers finished school, very few of us thought in terms of a career. We simply got a job and que sera sera. Many of us lucked into businesses such as advertising, construction, food services, trade work or product sales that we were totally untrained and unprepared for but we did our best, found a niche we liked and ultimately did well for ourselves.

For a further perspective on the issue, read this recent piece in The Globe and Mail by Mark Kingwell, Professor of philosophy at the University of Toronto. http://www.theglobeandmail.com/globe-debate/who-needs-harvard-send-us-your-best-and-brightest/article19887588/#dashboard/follows/

McJobs... I've had a few

When I heard that my husband's fourteen-year-old grandson had landed a part-time job working at Kernels I was suddenly filled with so much pride in him. Apart from being a good student and an active participant in Marc and Craig Kielburger's **Me to We** children's charity program, he's now a working man. I'm of the opinion that early work for young people is a good thing. It not only builds character but it helps them understand the value of earned money versus hand-outs. These are valuable life skills that ultimately contribute to young people becoming better citizens, better partners and better people. Canada is blessed with a large immigrant population and they seem more inclined to put their kids to work in the family business or elsewhere at an earlier age than most Canadians. These students frequently become high achievers in school and high achievers as adults.

My own life as a working girl began when I was eight years old. From 1955 to 1960 my parents owned one of two local taxis in our small Ontario town. It was my job to be home to answer the telephone when I wasn't in school, I would answer and dispatch calls to my mother or father on the two-way radio. They sold the business when I entered high school at the age of thirteen so by then I already had a resume with five years of working experience. I also had a steady supply of baby-sitting jobs charging the astronomical sum of twenty-five cents an hour, fifty cents after midnight. The summer I was thirteen and again when I was fourteen, I worked for a short time reeling yarn from 7:00 in the morning until 5:00 p.m. in the woolen mill where my Dad managed the carpet department. That experience was certainly incentive to stay and school and get an education.

Three years of waitressing as a high school student probably provided me with the best all-round experience. When I was fourteen I got a job as a carhop/waitress/short-order cook/dishwasher at the local drive-in burger joint where I continued to work part-time for the next three years until I left home. This was supplemented by my regular baby-sitting jobs and I taught Sunday school for several years. And these extra-curricular activities didn't absolve me from doing chores at home such as grass-cutting, shoveling snow and helping in the kitchen. At the age of sixteen I worked as a waitress at a summer resort off Manitoulin Island.

When I finished high school there were no significant permanent jobs in our town so leaving home at seventeen to work full-time in Toronto was a given. In fact it even seemed a bit easier because there was no more homework and no working weekends, at least in the beginning.

Over the years I've been a clerk-typist and cable assignor for Bell Canada, a sales representative for a cosmetics company in the lovely old Eaton's College Street store in Toronto, a secretary, receptionist, Corporate Marketing Manager for a multi-billion dollar company, civil servant under contract to the Federal government, communications rep for a software company, deliverer of diapers and adult incontinence products for a market research company, order-taker for a courier company and self-employed marketing consultant.

Nothing has ever been handed to me without my working for it. It has not always been easy but having a job from a young age made me fiscally responsible, independent and strong enough to be able to withstand all the challenges life throws in front of us. I'm always so delighted when I see young people with the initiative to go out and get themselves a job to help earn their keep. I know from experience that they're going to do okay in life. No matter how menial, difficult or unpleasant the work may be, they'll be acquiring valuable skills and resources to draw upon as they go through life. Whatever we're asked to do is a valuable learning experience, including respect for others who do it.

The various McJobs I've had over the years have left me with lifelong empathy and respect for the people who do those jobs. Fifty years after waitressing in high school I am and forever will be a generous tipper. When I'm tempted to become impatient with a retail sales associate, I remember what it's like to be on your feet on hard floors with a smile on your face for eight hours a day serving recalcitrant customers, making minimum wage surrounded by millions of dollars worth of merchandise I couldn't afford to buy – even with my employee discount. I have infinite respect for those blue collar workers in factories or doing manual labour in uncomfortable conditions, again for low wages. I think of the farm workers who pick the apples I eat, clean up after the pigs that become the pork tenderloin I enjoy and the millions of service workers who work nights and weekends so that I have the privilege to shop or eat in a restaurant at odd hours.

It's always fun to reminisce with other Boomers about the jobs we've had over the years and we're all in agreement that we're richer for those experiences. We compare war stories about working conditions and challenges that would be unacceptable and perhaps even illegal by today's standards. But these experiences are what fortified us. We learned about resilience, resourcefulness, perseverance, diplomacy, money management, responsibility and accountability. And it has provided us with an endless supply of stories to share over cold glasses of wine in the evening.

Our grandchildren are now working part-time at various McJobs to build up their own set of life skills and we're so proud of them. A friend's grandson works in the bakery of a supermarket. We have a golf-course groundskeeper, a construction worker, a restaurant hostess and now a professional corn popper. Whatever they learn through their experiences, however insignificant it may seem now, it will enrich their lives in so many ways they'll come to appreciate as they get older. Then, they too can share stories with their Gen X, Y and Z friends when they enjoy their well-earned retirement glasses of wine.

Chapter 8
Fashion

*If you're going to San Francisco,
be sure to wear some flowers in your hair
. . . Scott McKenzie, 1967*

The fashion world is a sea of don'ts

Fashion is a fickle mistress. And do not believe that the so-called fashion experts and stylists always know what they're talking about. I'm a huge fan of *The Marilyn Denis Show* but some of their fashion advice makes wonder what their fashion advisors have been smoking. Alexis Honce is an example of why Sears is going bankrupt. (And, she needs serious voice coaching to get rid of that ear-shattering nasal whine.) Marilyn, girlfriend, you have a great figure and we understand that you have waistline issues like the rest of us (especially me), but there has to be an alternative to wearing maternity tops every day. Peter Papapetrou is sometimes way-off in his choices and *CityLine's* Lisa Rogers is a saint for introducing me to FitFlops. Most of the time I trust Lynn Spence on *CityLine*. Sandra Pittana has a flair I adore but unfortunately I'm not tall and skinny enough to wear her taste in fashion. Oprah Magazine's Adam Glassman should stick with men's wear. Chatelaine sometimes gets it right but they still devote too much fashion space to twenty-somethings who probably don't even read *Chatelaine*.

If I were to listen to the latest fashion dictates I'd be wearing clunky fat-heeled pumps with a wide ankle strap that cuts the visual length of my leg, a short flouncy gathered skirt that accentuates my sixty-six-year old wrinkled knees and makes my torso look like a yeasty loaf of bread. A cropped top would be worn out over my skirt making me look even more tubular and if I'm really lucky it would have raglan sleeves further accentuating a horizontal dimension. Weekend wear would be geometric printed cuffed short-shorts with gladiator sandals—very flattering on less-than-perfect legs—and an oversize filmy floral blouse that makes me look like a walking funeral arrangement. On cooler days my knees would poke out through sloppy boyfriend jeans that play up the short dumpy look. And while we're at it, let's complete the ensemble with a couple of layered tank tops that highlight my bat-wing upper arms. Glimmer and sparkle my eyes with lots of iridescent eye shadow so every wrinkle and imperfection is spotlighted and colour my lips with a luscious fuscia lipstick that glows in the dark and makes my teeth look yellow and rotten.

I realize fashion magazines are only intended to inspire, that we're not supposed to go out and duplicate exactly what they feature. But we still look to them for *positive* inspiration and they deliver a disproportionate amount of ridiculousness. Where do these so-called stylists come from? They obviously have no understanding of the relationship between form and function. Stella McCartney, whose designs are always truly beautiful once said she designs with her (late) mother Linda in mind. Bless her heart. Sadly, her clothes are priced beyond the reach of ninety-nine-point-nine percent of us; same thing with Armani.

I've said it before and I'll *keep* saying it until someone listens. Baby Boomer Broads (killer B's) are a huge demographic. We have money to spend. We like looking great. We've made enough fashion mistakes in our lifetime to know the fashion don'ts when we see them and we're seeing plenty. When we make a mistake, we have caring girlfriends to intervene. Trust your instincts. And make yourself heard. Or call me. I have very strong opinions on the issue in case you haven't noticed.

Birkies Are back

All the fashion mags are currently featuring runway shows by big-name designers like Gucci with models wearing amped up Birkenstocks—yes, those comfortable earth-mother shoes once associated only with granola eaters and lesbians. My own reaction is when did they ever disappear? I'm reasonably cool and my Boomer girlfriends are über-cool and we've always loved to shop in the comfort of Birkenstocks, Mephistos or similar feet-friendly attire. We have about-town walking-out comfortable shoes and when our Birkies are past their prime they make great slippers for around the house.

My own personal favourite brand is FitFlops which are designed in the U.K. They're not cheap but I absolutely love them and over the past few years have accumulated six pairs. They caress and cushion the soles of your feet in all the right places and provide good arch support, an old-lady essential. Since I've been wearing them I've found it impossible to go out the door in anything but. Despite having a closet full of fabulous shoes which are hardly ever worn, I keep defaulting to my trusty FitFlops. I can motor for miles in them without getting blisters, rubbing, burning or cramping.

I highly suspect that Gucci, D&G and the other designers saw me and my trendsetter Boomer girlfriends out living life to the fullest in our comfies and figured they'd better jump on the bandwagon or miss out. As followers of fashion and a huge marketing demographic we can no longer be ignored. Hopefully it's just a matter of time now until designers start releasing waistbands and dropping hem lengths too. We're sick and tired of stupid fashions that cater only to the firm of flesh who weigh less than one hundred pounds and are six feet tall.

Don't be fooled by vanity sizing

There is no way on earth I'm a size six, despite the fact that my Not Your Daughter's Jeans and Club Monaco summer pants bear a label that says I am. Blame it on a sly marketing technique called vanity sizing. That's when clothing manufacturers cheat a bit by lowering the size number to make buyers feel better and more likely to purchase. At the present time I weigh many pounds more than I did in my heyday yet I'm two sizes smaller than thirty years ago? Math is definitely not my strong suit (I'm an extreme right-brainer; the left side is barely functional) but even I know that the numbers do not compute.

Back when I weighed what I wish I weighed now I consistently wore size eight or ten. Now that I'm older, fatter and have no waistline whatsoever, there is no way in hell I legitimately qualify to wear size six despite what the labels say. And after a lifetime of being a Medium (M) fit on top, one clothing designer has decreed I'm an Extra Small (XS). The only thing that has grown in size is my bra and bra sizes are so notoriously baffling no one relies on them anyway. My shoes are still size seven and probably always will be until I need extra room for industrial strength orthotics to keep me motoring. But then, I've never actually tried on a Jimmy Choo or Manolo Blahnik—maybe I'd be a dainty size five.

Vanity sizing is right up there with "sell the sizzle not the steak." Now that I'm older and perhaps have a few more bucks to spend on clothing, the designers are marketing to my desire to feel good and are regularly trimming my size tag to inflate my self-image. I know I'm not really a true size six but if I keep paying more for the higher-end clothing names someday I might believe it. There's another old marketing adage that says "Perception is reality". I'll bet if I opted for even more expensive lines, I'd be a size two. How could I resist?

In fact, buying more expensive clothes in fake teeny tiny sizes might ultimately be cheaper than all the money wasted on gym memberships, weight loss books, diet plans, and low-cal empty foods. And we'd probably look better too. Saving enough money to fit into a Stella McCartney or Armani size zero sounds like a goal worth striving for. And I'd never again have to say no to dessert.

The bottom line – wear only what fits your bottom perfectly. Disregard the numbers. They lie.

My heart goes out to Sarah Millican and everyone else who isn't a size zero

Jann Arden tweeted the other day about British comedienne Sarah Millican being trashed for wearing a particular dress while making a presentation at the BAFTA Awards (similar to the Gemini's in Canada and Oscar's in the U.S.) that was deemed by the pond scum who thinks they are the last word in fashion to be unflattering. For those of you who are not familiar with Sarah Millican, she's brilliantly funny, self-deprecating, pretty and genuinely nice. What more is necessary? I've had the good fortune to watch her guest a couple of times on The Graham

Norton Show on BBC Canada and immediately loved her personality. Sarah is a size eighteen-to-twenty which means she's not model-thin. Why should anyone care and make her feel ashamed because she's not a size zero.

On a similar note, I currently have a clipping from the newspaper on my desk saying that the La Perla boutique in New York (they sell lingerie) has recently pulled a mannequin from their store following a negative backlash from customers about the unrealistic depiction of the female form represented by the mannequin. It showed protruding ribs and hip bones which certainly looks nothing like any real human woman I know here in the first world.

This continuation of promoting anorexic female bodies as being the ideal must stop. In response to La Perla's faux pas, another lingerie manufacturer, Aerie has stepped up to the plate and promised to no longer Photoshop the models in their ads. That's a step in the right direction but they could go one better by employing only models with real-life soft and curvy bodies rather than rail-thin bone bags with weird globe-shaped surgically-enhanced breasts.

Dove brand soap products have been lauding realistic women for more than a decade now but the list of companies using this marketing approach is miniscule. The internet makes it easy to target the offenders and most of us have computers or smart phones. When you're unhappy with the media's representation of women, make yourself heard. The customers of La Perla spoke up and got the attention of the manufacturer. Women like Sarah Millican deserve better and we should make our support heard. Someday, someone will listen. I can't do this all by myself.

Lavish weddings – are they worth it?

Big, fancy over-the-top weddings, in my opinion are a waste of money. There—I've said it. That ought to ruffle a few feathers. While spending tens of thousands of dollars staging a giant wedding with a dozen attendants, white doves, horse-drawn carriages and hundreds of guests might be good revenue generators for the wedding planners, caterers and photographers/videographers, I question the ultimate value to the bride and groom not to mention the guests.

I've had two weddings. Both were modest affairs. The first one had about seventy-five guests and the second one, just over one hundred people. Each time I had only one attendant, and I made my own dress for the first one. Both of my weddings were stress-free. In fact, the second time around I was so busy at work I didn't even have time to order a cake so my best lady took care of it—a fantastic chocolate cake with real roses on it. She was so helpful she even took over the cutting of the cake at the reception. After a couple of glasses of wine I guess she thought I wasn't doing it right, so she pitched in. That's what girlfriends are for.

With the exposure of Bridezillas and other characters involved in planning and staging a wedding, it amazes me that this can truly be called the most wonderful day of your life. Tempers flare, disasters happen, relatives get snarky and more than fifty percent of the time, the marriage doesn't even last. The emphasis is frequently more on the wedding than on the marriage that follows, which should be a more important concern.

Many years ago I worked with a young lady who had one of the most jinxed weddings I've ever heard of. The night before the big day she went to the wedding planner with her four attendants to pick up their dresses. The attendants' dresses were far from being done and it was obvious they could not be completed in time. So, on Friday night before the rehearsal, the five of them blasted off to the mall seeking out a store that could produce four matching bridesmaids' dresses in size seven, nine, eleven and thirteen to wear the next day. Fortunately, Braemar (which is no longer in business) had just received a shipment that day and they were able to outfit all four attendants in matching dresses.

The wedding reception was held at a country lodge. When everyone arrived late in the afternoon, the wedding party discovered that the lodge had set up and planned a sit-down dinner for one hundred and fourteen people, not the one hundred and forty people requested. Everyone scrambled for extra chairs and tables while the kitchen stretched the food to feed an extra twenty-six mouths. When the bride and her new husband left the reception later that evening, they discovered their vehicle was stuck in the mud in the field where they'd parked next to the lodge. Still dressed in her wedding gown and new husband in his tux, they jointly had to dig in and push their vehicle out of the mud to leave.

When they reached the hotel on their wedding night, they discovered their room had not been guaranteed for late arrival and had been rented to someone else. So they went back to the bride's parents' home and she slept with her new husband in the little single bed she grew up in. To the best of my knowledge they're still married. Anyone who can withstand that much adversity on their wedding day can handle anything that comes after.

A successful businessman friend I once knew who had five daughters came up with what I thought was a brilliant solution to the runaway cost of weddings. He allotted each daughter a specific fixed dollar amount and instructed them that it was their choice as to whether they spent it on a big wedding or managed it differently. Either way, they would be given the same amount. Four of the five had modest weddings and used the leftover money toward a down payment on a house and the fifth opted for the big splashy affair.

Many people see a long list of wedding guests translating into a wedding gift bonanza including cash and cheques. Borrowing money to pay for a big gala on this assumption can backfire. Unless your friends and relatives are exceptionally well-off, it can be difficult to recoup the cost of a big production with a free bar and European crystal bonbonnières.

Destination weddings can also put unnecessary financial pressure on both the wedding party and guests. And, I have no doubt that many young women who have served as bridesmaids at multiple weddings would love to now have that cash in the bank. It requires a significant outlay to be in a wedding party to cover the cost of dresses, shoes, hairdo's, makeup the day-of and the cost of a wedding gift and numerous shower gifts. Thank you, but I think I'll just sit this one out. I'm saving for my own condo.

Second marriages often have more sensible weddings. Some of the loveliest and most meaningful weddings I've attended have been back-yard affairs with simple catered nibbles. But, ironically, second wives, because of improved economic circumstances often score bigger diamonds.

Back to my original assertion; I still think a small to mid-size wedding is the way to go.

Building my own oil cartel

Women's magazines and the cosmetics industry are always coming up with new and creative ways to separate us from our hard-earned toonies and loonies. Now that BB creams and CC creams have become old and boring (or reached critical mass as they say in the biz) they've unleashed new bait to lure us in—it's oil—and true to character I'm right at the front of the line. Just last night I ripped a page out of a magazine promoting *"Our first luxurious oil-infused lotion, Garnier Body Oil Beauty, Oil-infused Lotion for dry skin. Argan, macadamia, almond, rose, non-greasy, non-sticky. In our study, eighty percent agreed their skin has never looked so beautiful."* That does it—gotta get me some immediately!

This morning as I was applying Moroccan Argan Oil to the tips of my parched, high-lighted hair, I cast a glance around my medicine cabinet and started tallying up all the oils required to get me through the day.

1. Neutrogena Body Oil so my skin remains attached to my dermis and doesn't flake off.
2. Above-mentioned Moroccan argan oil for split ends.
3. Tea-tree oil for my eye-lashes (I'll explain later).
4. Cuticle oil for – well, you know.
5. Eardrop oil for when maintenance falls behind.
6. Bath oil

So far I've managed to stay clear of the new facial cleansing oils, oil-enriched shampoos, oil hair conditioners, primer oils and oil body washes. Then there are the dozens of other oils essential to daily living—fish oil capsules, olive, canola, grapeseed, sesame, coconut and sunflower oil for meal preparation. Not to mention diffusing oils to make my home smell like a spring meadow and special oils for my Lampe Bergère for the times I want to substitute one unpleasant smell for another.

Earlier this week I mentioned to my eye doctor that I was having a problem with dry, itchy eyes. He informed I could have invisible mites in my eyelashes that are causing the problem. The solution – tea tree oil of course. I purchased a packet of tee tree oil-based wipes to use on my closed eyelids twice a day for a month in hopes of returning my eyeballs from red to white.

I've already been using Oil of Olay serum for years and because I don't really look like a ninety-year old I guess it must be working. And we're not even taking into account all the oils that make my husband's world go 'round like WD-40, 10W-30 and various other mysterious oils lining the shelves of his workshop. I could go on but I think you get the picture.

Now that I've brought your attention to the industry's nasty strategy, perhaps we can resist the urge to go out and buy the latest and greatest. This is made easier by the fact the new Garnier Body Oil I covet doesn't seem to be available in Canada or U.S. yet. I saw the ad in RED, a British magazine. On the other hand, maybe I could try going on-line and having it sent . . .

What's the real cost of my mani-pedi

Once a month I treat myself to a mani-pedi at a local nail salon. I still regard the services as a treat since I didn't start indulging in such luxuries until I was in my fifties. Prior to that, every Sunday night an hour was allotted to giving myself a manicure to last the week. With the emergence of acrylic and gel nails these salons have popped up everywhere and although I have always eschewed artificial nails in favour of nature's own, mani-pedi's are as normal a part of maintenance for everyone now as a trip to the hairdressers.

My local salon in Mississauga is staffed by no less than a dozen young Asian women. Walk-ins are convenient and easy with no waiting. Sitting at the front door manning the cash register is Papa-san whom I presume is the proprietor. When a client walks in he summons a free attendant and the work begins. Now that I'm getting creaky it's lovely to have someone attend to my feet. Oh, the decadence of a scented soak in a foot jacuzzi followed by pumicing and buffing of the soles of my feet, filing of nails, tidying up cuticles, a creamy foot and leg massage and finally the layers of base coat, two applications of polish and a top coat. The job done by these professionals is far superior to what I do myself and I leave feeling quite lovely.

As I'm sitting there in the massaging chair, I've observed some pretty disgusting sights. During one visit I witnessed the pedicurist stripping large dead calloused slices off the soles of the feet of the woman in the next chair that reminded me of peeling a potato. Just a couple of weeks ago there was a man with ugly dark-coloured feet with callouses and formations that made me think of Jim Carrey's pedicure that required a chain saw, belt sander and blow torch in Dumb & Dumber. I'll give the man the benefit of the doubt. Perhaps he was diabetic. Not a fun job for the attendant.

The only part of this process that makes me uncomfortable is the nature of the working conditions for the young women who perform these services. They are consistently polite but never seem happy. Walking in and requesting services leaves me feeling as if I'm entering a Bangkok brothel. Are these ladies relatives of the attendant? How are they paid? Are they paid at all or are they there to "learn English"? Not all salons are like this but there does appear to be a pattern and it worries me. While I enjoy getting a mani-pedi for between thirty and forty dollars, how can they pay staff and overheads at such low margins? In more sophisticated salons I've paid as much as fifty-five dollars for a pedicure alone (manicure extra) but these establishments always require an appointment and I honestly cannot justify the extra forty dollars for the same result.

My respect for these young women and the work they do means I'm a very generous tipper. I still can't help wondering about their personal lives. Are they happy? Do they have plans for the future? I'll just have to keep wondering. They're working at earning an honest living and that is commendable. As someone fortunate enough to be born in North America, our choices and options have always been much more wide-ranging than if we'd been born elsewhere in the world. I only hope that the young lady performing my mani-pedi is being paid fairly and now has the same choices and options the rest of us enjoy.

March madness explained

Please tell me I'm not the only person in the world who thought March Madness was about special annual retail sales—like Black Friday.

For weeks leading up to the big event and for the duration, I kept waiting for the flyers from my favourite retailers to arrive in my mailbox. With visions of bargain-priced sugar plums dancing in my head I couldn't wait to hit the mall to stock up on half-price underwear and my favourite jeans. Surely all the cosmetics companies would be having extra-special promotions with yummy shades of lipstick in their giveaways.

Excitement turned to disappointment when the media started talking sports in the same sentence as March Madness. My suspicions were confirmed when I asked my husband who gently explained that the "real meaning" of March Madness was the narrowing down of sports teams competing for ranking in their respective cups—as in athletic. Yes, Virginia. There is a Santa Claus but not in March.

Let's burn our bras – again

As I get older and more crotchety, I'm less tolerant of things that annoy me. I compare today's styles in high heels to the twenty-first century's version of foot binding. I'd now like to include bras in that category. All Boomer Broads agree that the "girls" need support—we have no problem with that. But why does that support have to be designed solely for the eye of the beholder not the wearer. Why do bras have to be itchy, scratchy, binding, pinching and protruding? Whoever said the girls have to be separately displayed and in an upright position, in see-through lace structurally engineered with no consideration for comfort.

In my younger days I could get away with fitted camisoles alone so I didn't have to deal with underwire pinch or slippage. There was no pressure on my ribcage and no clasps or other accoutrements to detract from a smooth tee shirt. Then, menopause hit, along with a few extra pounds and my upper body has been a work in progress ever since.

I *hate* wearing a bra – plain and simple. When I've been out all day, I can't wait to get home and rip the thing off. I gave up on underwire because they were always pinching and shifting. But even the wireless soft cups put uncomfortable pressure on your ribcage and across the back. Au naturel feels so much better. Many stretch athletic bras approach some level of comfort but still put vice-like pressure on the ribcage and back.

I once fell for the myth at all my problems would be solved once I invested in a good quality, properly-fitted European bra. So I dropped two hundred dollars on a delicate black lace number, made in France. When I test drove it in the store it felt fine but after a couple of hours on the highway of life my upper body felt like it was being attacked by scorpions. Most of the European bras place the straps on the outer edge of your shoulders. Unless you're built like a linebacker, those straps are constantly sliding off.

And don't tell me to get properly fitted. Every place I go to gives me a different number and cup size. There's no consistency in the design and manufacturing of bras or in the measurement techniques. The ultimate design for comfort for me is a full tank-style top with extra Lycra lining across the bust area to keep the girls in place but not necessarily separate and pointing skyward. I have no objection to a uniboob although I seem to be in the minority. I've surveyed my inner circle of Boomer Broads for their position on the issue and here's what they had to say:

"I have not been able to get away without a bra – ever! Mine are not conducive to anything lacy, stretchy or flimsy. I have no idea what Victoria's Secret is because I'm left out of her *shop*. She doesn't carry big girl sizes and I would be daunted to shop there even if they did."

"Closer to 'au naturel' at my age and stage would just be painful. There's more to this than A, B and C. My alphabet has D-E and who knows, we may get to F someday. My size comes in no pretty, practical designs – just the standard classic that comes in three colours and goes on sale once a year, when I stock up. I like to keep things simple and don't allow my cup to runneth over."

Another friend covers the whole spectrum. She enjoys the au naturel feeling around home but likes to get tarted up in matching lacy, pretty pantie and bra sets for special occasions.

Whatever our choices, I have not met a single person who is a bra fan. They're expensive, for the most part uncomfortable and the cause of much frustration. It's hard to believe we were once so proud to shed our little-girl undershirts for our first training bra. Little did we know we'd spend the rest of our lives in binding servitude? There has to be a better way. I'd burn them all but I have too much invested in them. And then, not only would the "girls" collapse but so would our entire economy and I don't want to be responsible for that. So I'll just soldier on, complaining and grumbling about it 'til death do us part, at which time I'll be blissfully free.

Hair Today, Gone Tomorrow

Here baby, there mama
Everywhere daddy daddy . . . hair!

Hair is a very complicated business whatever our type of hair – dark, fair, straight, curly, thick, and thin. Whatever we have, we want the opposite. Then there are the thousands of products available to supposedly give us the hair we've always dreamed of. Growing up, my whole family used the same eight-ounce glass bottle of Halo shampoo, until it was gone. Then we bought a replacement bottle at the grocery store. We'd never heard of conditioners. It wasn't until a girlfriend and I waitressed for a summer at a resort off Manitoulin Island in 1964 that I was introduced to Tame Crème Rinse. The other girls working there were from Richmond Hill, Ontario, obviously sophisticated city types who knew about these things. That was just part of my education that summer, but that's another story.

Today, a trip to the drugstore or beauty salon to purchase shampoo requires a degree in chemical engineering and Olympian stamina just to navigate the shampoo aisle. The shelves stretch for miles and feature multiple variations of multiple brands and products. For example, Head & Shoulders alone offers the following different formulas for shampoo:

Classic Clean leaves hair looking clean and dandruff-free

Citrus Breeze created with citrus essence created for oily hair

Refresh – added natural menthol gives a cooling soothing feeling

Ocean Lift invigorates your hair and scalp

Extra Volume adds body and bounce while making your hair easy to control

Smooth & Silky smoothed your hair and makes it soft and manageable

Dry Scalp Care with moisturizers soothes the scalp

Sensitive Care hypoallergenic formula developed specifically for sensitive scalps

Hair Endurance for thicker looking hair

Clinical Strength formulated to fight persistent, severe dandruff

Itchy Scalp Care helps soothe itchy scalps associated with dandruff

Now they also have a men's hair product line as well. And this is just *one brand*. Oh, for the days of choosing between good old Halo or Breck shampoo. Depending on whatever crisis I am currently experiencing, I have shampoo for colour-treated hair, dandruff treatment, de-gunking formula, clarifying shampoo, sulphate and paraben-free, organic, just-smells-good shampoo, shampoo and conditioner combo, prescription formula for itchiness, volumizing shampoo, thickening shampoo, gentle baby formula, curl enhancer, and psychic colour-smart shampoo for blondes only. They all come in separate bottles. And they all have corresponding conditioners in separate bottles. And I need them all. Styling products require even more bottles – thickeners, volumizers (I still haven't figured out the difference so I buy both just to be on the safe side), mousse, gels (spray, liquid and gel formulas), colour toners, deep treatments, foams and shine enhancers.

It took me several tries before I finally scored the right blow dryer. There's a big difference in how half a dozen seemingly similar 1875 kilowatt blow dryers actually perform. There are even special serums and conditioning creams for taming the blow dryer effect. Some people use a curling iron and I keep several for emergencies. Once again, several barrel sizes are required depending on the length of the hair and the size of the curl you want to achieve. Flat irons are employed by those individuals who want to un-curl their hair. And now they even have a curling iron that sucks your hair into its secret chamber and spirals it into glamorous curls not achievable by previous methods. Finally – to spray or not to spray? If I do I risk looking like a helmet-head. If I don't, the entire project will collapse and I've squandered hours of time and product. To hormone or not to hormone; to grow it out or keep it short. Much as I'd love to have a flouncy, flirty bob like Cameron Diaz, my hair type restricts me to short.

And now I'm going bald – pretty soon all I'll need is a squirt of Windex for that fresh look. That should simplify my hair issues. My friend Terry says that when I die, she's going to have inscribed on my tombstone, *"Finally, she's stopped complaining about her hair."*

Think I'll go have another glass of wine. That always makes me feel beautiful.

Shame on Joe Fresh

Ordinarily I'm a huge fan of the Joe Fresh brand. They offer affordable, fashionable clothing with quick turnover of designs. They let me down however when I saw their most recent commercial for children's clothing. As I was watching the television the other night, a Joe Fresh commercial aired that made me very uncomfortable. It showed a number of small children dressed in adult-style clothing performing adult-style choreography. Their provocative moves were meant to be cute but struck me as being sexually exploitive of children – and I am by no means a prude. It would have probably not bothered me so much if it weren't for the fact my husband, watching the same commercial commented, "That's a terrible commercial" – guy-speak for he didn't like it either. The ensuing discussion confirmed that he immediately had the same reaction I did – the ad made sexual objects of children. So I wasn't imagining it. I tried to find the commercial on the internet but could only find a picture from it on the Joe Fresh Facebook page.

If you agree, e-mail them to let them know. I did. https://www.joefresh.com/

How to rock on

I've just finished watching the most fascinating British documentary that came to me via *The Huffington Post*. It's about fashionable women in their seventies, eighties and nineties and how they view life. What an inspiration for Boomer Broads like ourselves. Make yourself a nice cup of tea or coffee, or pour yourself a lovely glass of wine, allow a bit of time (I think it's almost an hour) and tune in. It'll put a smile on your face and you'll feel much better after. http://www.huffingtonpost.ca/2013/11/25/fabulous-fashionistas_n_4338067.html

Preparing Part One
of my twenty-five year plan

During my forty-odd years in the corporate world, I would periodically set goals for my professional and personal life. This helped me focus and move forward instead of just rolling along with the status quo. Now that I'm a sixty-six-year old retired Boomer Broad, setting goals requires a different set of metrics. Instead of "Be promoted to Vice-President by age forty-two" or "Have mortgage paid off by age fifty," my challenges now include things like "figure out how to make money last until I can no longer count to ten" or "Send Tim Horton's a fan letter about their steeped tea." Today's goals include "Get oil changed" and "Do nails."

Coming from a family with a history of long life-spans, I figure I'm good for another thirty years which means almost one-third of my entire life is still ahead of me. So a plan to make best use of those years is now in the making. Part 1 of my plan includes presentation. How am I going to present my shrinking, wrinkling, creaking old body to the world? The way I look at it, I see three possible choices.

The first one is the path of least resistance. If I take this route, I'll be wearing beige polyester pants with an elastic waist and white fifty-fifty cotton blend granny pants underneath, print blouses in subdued floral patterns and pilled cardigans with a snotty Kleenex up the sleeve. My shoes will be Soft-Moc slip-ons in black or beige with thin white ankle socks or beige knee-highs with reinforced toes for extra mileage. My hair will be au naturel and softly permed every three months. Wardrobe staples will include pink and blue sweatshirts with teddy bears or strawberries embroidered around the neckline. I'll have a running account at Alison Daley or Tan-Jay. Easy-peasy stress-free dressing.

The second option is the Iris Apfel one. She's the ninety-two-year old New Yorker regularly featured in *Vogue* in huge black-framed glasses, enormous brightly-coloured jewellery and clothing that looks like it was lifted from the costume rack of the Metropolitan Opera. I absolutely love her look and admire her lady-balls but I'm not sure I could pull it off. Much as I'd like to try I'd end up looking like I'm wearing a Halloween costume.

I think my chosen path is somewhere in between and toward that end I've recently purchased a pair of biker boots that I adore. When I wear those boots with black skinny pants, a black jacket and my red and black animal print scarf I feel absolutely invincible. I also bought an Alexander McQueen silver skull pendant to wear over black sweaters or white blouses with skinny jeans. I have to make up for those conservative years in my twenties when I should have been dressing more provocatively and showing off the firm thin body I naively thought I'd have forever.

As I get older and less tolerant of life's bumps in the road, I'm becoming more resolved to be true to myself. I no longer worry what other people think of me and that carries over to what I wear and what I say or do. Without hurting anyone, I intend to concentrate on enjoying every day on my own terms.

Which brings me to another of my favourite things. If you notice someone sweeping past you on the street in a suffocating haze of floral perfume, that'll be me. Too bad if you have allergies. I have a weakness for pretty fragrances in pretty bottles. They say that as we age our olfactory senses diminish so I figure more generous splashings will be needed so I can fully enjoy my juice du jour. When people are falling down on the street from asphyxiation in my wake, I'll hobble happily along in my biker boots to meet my bitch posse for afternoon tea and trashing-talking current fashion.

When Rita McNeil passed away she requested that her ashes be buried in a teapot – or two if necessary. Don't 'ya just love that? As a serious tea drinker myself I thought that sounded like a splendid idea.

Then a friend suggested I should be buried in my favourite Louis Vuitton purse that EllisDon gave me when I retired. That's an even more splendid idea as the one thing I love more than tea is purses. That's almost worth looking forward to.

There's no business like shoe business

Who doesn't get a high from new shoes? When I first bring them home, I tenderly take them out of the box, smell the leather, stroke the smooth soles and carefully place them at just the perfect angle on the dining room table or end table in the livingroom where I can admire them like precious works of art. I may even move them to my bedside table so they will be the first things I see when I wake up in the morning. By the end of wearing them on the first day, however, my heels and baby toes are usually plastered in Band-Aids, the balls of my feet are screaming "fire" and my back gave up around ten o'clock in the morning.

Back in the "olden days" in the sixties and seventies when I was in my twenties I wore high heels exclusively every day to work. For many years I lived downtown and walked or more often ran to work, as I'm not a morning person and was usually late. Just like the Post Office before they went union, neither wind, nor rain, nor sleet nor hail could keep me from my high-heeled rounds. I clearly remember envying the brogue-wearing men in my office who never had to cope with foot discomfort and burning balls – of the feet, that is.

Now that I am *in* my sixties I marvel that my feet are not crippled. Today I can barely totter through a holiday party in three-inch heels without wincing in pain. The other day I was shopping in Holt Renfrew and I spotted a fresh young sales associate wearing the most orgasmic pair of high-heeled python pumps. Oh, for the good old days. I told her to enjoy them because some day she was going to be like me wearing Menopause Mephistos with industrial-strength arch supports. Of course, she didn't understand. I didn't either at that age. At a recent

Celebration of Life event I had to stand for about three hours in dress shoes and suffered with painful back spasms for days after.

Heels are growing increasingly higher and spikier. Shoe designers are predominantly men. Their designs are truly meant to be admired as works of art – not worn and walked in. Oprah and Marilyn Denis are just two media Boomer broads who readily admit that the only time they wear the killer heels is for the sixty minutes they're actually on the air, walking to the set in flats. Five-inch heels should be illegal. It's a form of abuse right up there with Chinese foot-binding and that's been illegal for more than a century.

Unfortunately, it is our own fault for submitting to this tyranny. Shoe designers should be made to walk in their shoes. I'd love to see Jimmy Choo, Franco Sarto or Christian Louboutin being forced to wear their designs eight or ten hours a day for even a week. Then watch the designs change. And the prices are pure usery. A thousand dollars for a pair of Valentino high-heeled sandals!!! Give me strength.

Let's show some solidarity ladies. Pick pretty but wearable. Surely they can design comfy shoes in saucy animal prints with fun embellishments and hidden arch supports that still project that we're hot, current and sexy. We're Boomers. We're a demographic with serious buying power. Make yourself heard in the shoe stores. Storm The Bastille, Boomer Broads.

Think I'll go and put on my new Geox biker boots and strut the town. I'm lookin' good and feelin' fine. Let's rock n' roll.

Walkin' tall with my Louis

Whoever said looks don't count was lying. And whoever said first impressions do count was absolutely bang on. Perversely, this has proven to apply to the purses we carry. When I retired, instead of presenting me with a boring gold watch, my employer surprised me with my very first and still favourite designer purse. I'd carried a picture of it around with me for weeks before I left and had planned to blow my entire last paycheque on it.

It's a Louis Vuitton Manhattan bag, which, by the way is no longer made so to me it's extra special. It's the epitome of everything I could ever want in a handbag. It's not overly big or small and has two latched front pockets for my car keys and cell phone. When I walk into a store I feel like and am treated like a "somebody". It shouldn't be that way but it is. Based on the first impression created by my handbag, sales staff immediately assume I can afford whatever they're peddling. They treat me with special attention as visions of commissions dance through their heads, while missing out on the real potential commissions from purses of lower status with probably more genuine purchasing power inside. Purses do not make the Boomer but they sure can make her feel like a million bucks.

Grasping at skinny straws for solutions

Boomer broads are never at a loss for excuses about we're always a few (or more) pounds overweight: I'm big-boned; it's hereditary; it's my thyroid; I don't have time to exercise, or simply, I just love cookies and ice-cream. Well, my dears, your Boomerbroadcaster has come through with the definitive word on why **it's not our fault**. It all has to do with city planning. You see, a recent research study of twenty-four cities in California by several university engineering professors concluded that the reason we're all becoming obese and diabetic is because guys like Le Corbusier decided in the 1930s that people would be happier and healthier if our cities were more park-like. That meant no more efficient and boring street grids that connected us to stores and workplaces in the least amount of time. Instead, it was deemed that twisty, winding, wide avenues and cul de sacs would be more conducive to our well-being.

The result of that brilliance is that in North America it now takes us longer to get anywhere and cars are such a necessity that our entire economy has been built upon building, selling and driving cars. Unlike densely-populated cities in Europe where people walk much more than we lazy North Americans do, our residential communities are located on the perimeter of working areas. Living and working spaces are completely separated and lovely though that may be it has created generations of fatties with an increasing litany of health issues resulting from being unable to walk to the corner store without starting the car and driving to get there.

Growing up in small-town Ontario in the fifties, we rarely went anywhere in the car. My parents walked to their factory jobs. Everyone walked or biked to school except farm kids but their farm chores were usually completed before they hopped onto that bus at 7:30 a.m. Attendance at Brownies, Girl Guides, Sunday school, birthday parties, babysitting jobs, swimming lessons, summer jobs and all other events was always on foot, unaccompanied by adults. There were neighbourhood stores in the front of someone's house every few blocks and we were always being sent to the store for last-minute quarts of milk, loaves of bread or a brick of neopolitan ice-cream for dessert. Malls didn't exist in the fifties and early sixties so we shopped locally in our small town, on foot. How far we've fallen.

So you see, we can thank Le Corbusier for leading our city planners astray and we can thank those university professors for explaining why we can't lose weight. I suppose we could all move to Paris where our butcher, baker, wine store and greengrocer would all be around the corner and we could walk to everything. I rather like that idea but I'm probably too old to become bilingual and I'm not about to take up smoking. I do think, however, our population and our city planners are starting to realize that driving ninety minutes to and from work each day is not the best use of resources on so many levels. It's probably too late to start ripping up our cities to make the necessary changes but at least we can encourage them to start pouring money into public transit. That would at least require us to walk to the bus stop, climb up and down stairs to transfer to the subway and carry our groceries home in shopping bags.

The problem remains. I'm too old and too fat to live in Paris. Our city planners are ignoring the needs of seniors and baby boomers in terms of transportation and accommodation, and ongoing cutbacks in healthcare are jeopardizing any chance I might have of losing weight by making me pay for liposuction. I can only hope those city planners have an efficient plan for transporting my fat old corpse when I have a heart attack behind the wheel of my SUV on my way home from the bake shop at rush hour. If they wouldn't listen to neighbourhood advocate Jane Jacobs, what hope do I have?

Boomer beauty 101 – circa 1965

The other day as I was sorting and cleaning out my copious supplies of pricey cosmetics and toiletries it occurred to me I could open my own Shoppers Drug Mart, and I'm not proud of it. That caused me to reflect on how this insidious habit began in 1965. I was living in Willard Hall, a girls' residence at 20 Gerrard Street East in downtown Toronto. My move into Willard Hall at the age of seventeen marked the beginning of new adulthood, when I left home and began working for the telephone company. It was a jumping-off point for small-town virgins coming to seek their fortunes in the big city. I was now exposed to sophisticated city girls who knew things—things I'd never even heard about before. This included insights into fashion and beauty that were considered frivolous and vain where I came from. Allow me a trip down memory lane with some of my Boomer friends as we remember the way it was.

All of a sudden I was living with girls who wore makeup, knew how to create amazing hairdos, spent their wages on the latest British street fashions and even purchased fashion magazines. My girlfriend Linda who worked with me at Ma Bell was taking modelling classes at The Walter Thornton Agency so she was particularly au courant. Linda introduced me to my first compact of Max Factor blusher with the little brush. At three ninety-nine it was an atrocious price when my weekly salary before taxes was only fifty-five dollars. But the effect it had on Linda's cheekbones when she expertly brushed it across her cheeks was impressive so I had to get one.

The influence of all the girls living at Willard Hall was inspiring. Diane, who roomed across the hall first made me aware of the importance of lingerie. After the release of Georgie Girl, Lynn Redgrave's iconic 1966 debut movie, she went on the hunt at the Evangeline store at Yonge and Carlton Streets looking for a mini-length demi-slip (bra and slip combo) worn by Charlotte Rampling in the movie. In fact, Charlotte Rampling's character was a totem for those of us from small towns with straw still stuck to our new platforms. Was it possible that someone outside our residence was actually seeing their lingerie? Ah! The sexual revolution was happening.

Jean Shrimpton was my idea of perfection. She modelled for only a few years and retired to obscurity in the early seventies. A few of the girls living in our residence were attending hairdressing school and came into the dining room sporting the most incredible haircuts and trendy do's. One particularly exotic creature, Nina was model-like tall, lean and beautiful. Nina's hair was coloured the richest shade of chestnut I'd ever seen and she'd bravely had her straight, shiny hair cut into an asymmetrical version of the Sassoon five-point cut that was all the rage at that time.

My room-mate Liz and I had been successfully and economically cutting each other's hair into neat blunt cuts but decided to throw a bit of colour into the mix. Off we went to Kresgie's on Yonge Street where we each purchased a box of Clairol's Nice 'N Easy in Strawberry Blonde for a dollar ninety-nine. Thus began a life-time of root touchups every six weeks. I never did roll my hair in orange juice cans or rinse it in a mixture of sugar and water for extra holding power, but I certainly knew girls who did both.

Before long I was applying Cover Girl liquid makeup and Mabelline Great Lash mascara with the best of them. The white lipstick we used as a base for other colours of lipstick to prevent them from turning red doubled as under-eye concealer. In fact, lipstick was also used as blusher and at a much more agreeable price than Max Factor's blusher— a two-for. By watching the other girls in our common washroom, I quickly absorbed more secrets and tricks to putting your best face forward. Beauty products were less abundant then and we were very careful about how we spent our pennies so improvisation was essential. In the sixties we used Mabelline's stubby red eyebrow pencils for shaping our brows and it wasn't until the seventies that we plucked our eyebrows into extinction. Eye-liner came in the form of a little dry cake of Revlon eyeliner that we applied with a wet brush. Nail polish was a single bottle of Revlon's Café au Lait with no top coat, no base coat and definitely no regular trips to the mani-pedi salon—it was strictly do-it-yourself.

The girls who were being subsidized by their parents (I was definitely not one of them and neither were my girlfriends) would wear expensive L'Air du Temps or White Shoulders fragrance. Since I could never afford such an extravagance, at lunchtime I'd zip off to the little drugstore in the office building on Edward Street behind mine where I'd generously spritz myself with pricier scents from the counter-top testers. I practically asphixiated my co-workers when I returned from lunch in a haze of lily-of-the-valley or Persian lilac. But I did manage to scrape together the funds for the smallest-size bottle of Estée Lauder's Youth Dew which seemed very classy and exotic.

One day I noticed the girl at the next sink in the washroom scouring her face with a sandpaper-like compound called Snap which, when mixed with water was originally designed to remove axle grease from mechanics' hands. She said her doctor had recommended it for her acne. Naturally I got on that bandwagon too and followed it up with Bonne Belle's Ten-O-Six Lotion, an astringent in the days before it was called toner. Moisturizer hadn't yet entered our beauty regime. It's amazing I have any epidermis left.

Boomer girls in the sixties washed our hair twice a week and when our bangs got oily we hit them with the giant fuzzy puff of bath powder that always sat on our dresser. As a bonus, it added volume too. We also kept a little plastic container of Nuvola dry shampoo to shake into our roots in emergencies. Nuvola was like a mixture of talcum powder and cornstarch but it achieved the desired effect. It cost one dollar and twenty-nine cents which was a bit pricey but the little plastic lavender-capped container lasted forever.

Sun tanning was de rigueur and we faithfully slathered our bodies in Johnson's baby oil with a few drops of iodine mixed in to enhance the frying properties. The resulting blistering sunburns were diligently treated with Noxzema until our skin fell off in sheets. The resulting blotchy tan was not attractive but more importantly, we're now paying for our sins by seeking out expensive laser and lightening procedures to restore our damaged skin.

Every night we slept with a partial or entire head of hair encased in brush rollers to beef-up the bouffant. Bangs were scotch-taped to our foreheads to keep them straight and in place. Blow dryers had not yet been invented so twice a week we sat for an hour or so under an inflatable plastic hood that blew hot air through a plastic hose into our rolled-up "do". Long, luscious locks like Jean Shrimpton's were the goal.

Back to the future – 2014. How could some simple makeup essentials and a teasing comb turn into the horror of consumerism that has become my bathroom cupboard today? Looking back, I should have stuck with my original formula: wash my face and body with a single bar of Dial soap; baby shampoo for my hair; Tame Crème Rinse; set, dry hair; spritz on a bit of French Formula hair spray; touch of Cover Girl face powder to hide the sun damage; a single eyebrow pencil to fix my earlier plucking disasters; a couple of swipes of cheap mascara and we're good to go. If I could follow that regime I'd be able to live in a smaller house and would save thousands of dollars on false promises. But what would I do with the bags and bags of products collecting dust in my cupboards. Too bad consignment stores don't take slightly used bottles of hair products, face and body moisturizers, makeup, nail polish, cleansers, serums and toiletries.

Being a single girl back in the olden days, the swingin' sixties was an incredible pleasure and a unique experience I love sharing with my Boomer girlfriends. Come to think of it, upon reflection I'm pretty sure some of those Willard Hall girls weren't even virgins.

Chapter 9
Books

I Want To Be A Paperback Writer,
. . . The Beatles, 1966

So Many Books, So Little Time

Every time I read a good book I feel like I've discovered something on par with the key to perpetual motion. I immediately want to share the good news with the entire world and for all my friends to read it so we can discuss it and marvel over its brilliance. I've ordered copies of *Lots of Candles, Plenty of Cake* by Anna Quindlen to be sent to some of my Boomer Broad friends. I just know that they'll read it with wide smiles of recognition on their faces as they relate to the descriptions of the pleasures and perils of being in our sixth or seventh decade. And if they don't – well, I try not to think about that.

Discovering the literary genius of a writer I can relate to brings me so much pleasure I can feel the excitement rise as I turn the pages to reveal new delights. Such was the case with "The Baby Boom" by P.J. O'Rourke that I finished reading a couple of weeks ago. Now I want to read all his books. And similarly I now want to read everything ever written by Anna Quindlen. But I already have a pages-long spreadsheet of other books I want to read. Then there are the eighteen magazines I subscribe to every month. Reading has become the focus of my retirement after not having the time to indulge myself during my forty years in the corporate world.

Free access to downloading e-books from Mississauga Library continues to be a marvel to me. I put my name on waiting lists on-line for best-sellers and miraculously one day I receive an e-mail that the book is ready for me to borrow. And I don't even have to leave the comfort of my living room La-Z-Girl. A pot of tea, a President's Choice oatmeal chocolate chip cookie and some reading material in my hand, my dog snoozing in my lap, and my honey watching football in the next room with his headphones on – life just doesn't get any better.

French women get it

Contrary to author Mireille Guiliano's assertion in her book titled French Women Don't Get Facelifts, they actually do —although not going to the unnatural extremes common in North America.

Having read her earlier best-seller, French Women Don't Get Fat, I was curious to see what she could add to my quest for knowledge about achieving eternal beauty.

The book was full of the usual good advice about eating healthy, natural foods, exercising the body and nourishing the mind and spirit. She covered all the usual bases including basic wellness, hair, makeup, clothes and of course, shoes and bags. Anecdotal information about her friends and their beauty habits made for an interesting read.

With homes in New York, Paris and Provence she moves in rather different circles than most of us. As the former spokesperson for Champagne Veuve Clicquot and senior executive at LVMH (Louis Vuitton) as well as CEO of Clicquot, Inc., she obviously has the resources, the motivation, the budget and the essential raw materials to package herself to her best advantage. The result is the best she can be.

While I try to be the best I can be much of the time, I'll never achieve Guiliano's level of je ne sais quois. I'll forever be several pounds overweight, never acquire that perfect once-in-a-lifetime flattering haircut and I'll always be inclined to be a bit lazy. I do however possess the ability to recognize great shoes when I see them. Guiliano claims to wear only four pairs of shoes—Ferragamos. While I do not have the resources to buy her favourite brand, her second-best choice for comfort unearthed a brand name new to me and not stratospherically out of my price range.

United Nude shoes are designed by a Dutch architect Mattijs van Bergen and are available on-line, sometimes at reduced prices. Just Google "United Nude." I've always favoured clothes and jewelry that are architecturally inspired. That's why I absolutely love Tiffany's new T-jewelry collection which short of winning the lottery I'll never be able to afford. I'm attracted to the odd angles, geometric designs and quirky compositions. Happily, I found a pair of United Nude shoes on-line that I absolutely loved and were manageable financially so I ordered them (free shipping).

French women may not get fat and they may forgo facelifts but they most certainly get shoes. And now I'm going to get them too. Can't wait for that FedEx truck to ring my bell. Maybe my new shoes will help me speak better French. It's worth a try. N'est çe pas?

This #GIRLBOSS has her sh$# together

The first time I heard the name Sophia Amoruso was during a radio interview when she was promoting her new book, *#Girlboss*. This twenty-something young woman was describing her path to becoming owner of a highly-successful on-line retail fashion business called *Nasty Gal*. Her business smarts were remarkable for someone so young and my heart sang when she outlined her advice based on lessons learned that were so in-line with my own that I couldn't wait to read her book.

Amoruso was the rebellious only child of baby boomers who grew up in San Francisco. Diagnosed with ADD, she was always swimming against the current and attended a different school nearly every year. Never a conscientious or cooperative student, she distinguished herself by wearing strange vintage clothing and generally resisting all efforts by her parents and teachers to conform.

Leaving home before finishing high school, Amoruso bounced around living the life of a young vagrant who managed to keep herself fed and clothed by dumpster diving and shoplifting. With a peculiar knack for sourcing and selling unique vintage clothing found at thrift and charity shops, she started selling her finds on eBay. This was the beginning of her understanding of the basic principles of work and reward, profit and loss.

Before long, she set up her own website for selling vintage merchandise and like most beginning entrepreneurs she did everything herself including buying, repairing, cleaning, merchandising, packing, and shipping her fashion finds herself. She soon recruited a friend to help and grew her business to three hundred and fifty employees and annual sales in excess of one hundred million dollars in vintage and new clothing sales shipped to customers around the world.

Still only in her twenties, Amoruso is an example worth paying attention to. Because she had no credit, her entire business was built on whatever income she generated, her own hard work, a genuine love for what she was doing and turning the profits she made back into the business. There were no well-researched business plans, bank loans, fancy offices or early investors involved.

I loved the book. I endorse her philosophy. And I highly recommend her book. She's a kind of anti-Sheryl-Sandberg example in that she had no educational or financial advantages. The business she created confirms that a successful career based on hard work, an original idea and perseverance can be achieved. Good fortune is earned and Amoruso used her own no-cost resources to become her own boss and a successful one to boot.

Heather O'Neill bangs it home

Waiting more than two months to download Heather O'Neill's new book, The Girl Who Was Saturday Night from the library was worth the wait. I have a soft spot for Canadian authors and I thoroughly enjoyed O'Neill's debut novel Lullabies for Little Criminals enormously. She writes about the grittier side of life in Montreal, Quebec through the eyes of a young teenager in her first book and a twenty-year old in The Girl Who Was Saturday Night. The main character, Noushcka is the twin sister of Nicholas. They are the illegitimate children of a legendary nineteen-seventies Québécois folksinger Étienne Tremblay and his one-night stand with a fourteen-year old girl. The twins were abandoned at birth to their paternal grandparents who raised them in the rough Boulevard Saint-Laurent neighbourhood on the island in Montreal.

An English teacher would be impressed with O'Neill's frequent and graphic use of similes and metaphors. Her descriptions of cats are sensitive and painterly, "A calico cat was sleeping on its back, like a girl in grey stockings with her skirt pulled up over her hips."

Twins Nouskcka and Nicholas were raised during their impressionable teenage years by their aging grandfather, Loulou on his own following the death of his wife. They drop out of school and despite Loulou's best efforts they inevitably screw up.

Both twins are precocious and Noushcka in particular displays potential for rising above her circumstances. She is intelligent and is trying to earn a better education at night school so she can become a writer. Predictably, they hang around with the wrong people and get into trouble as a result of being irresponsible and emotionally immature. Like many twins, they share a special psychic bond and feel lost and diminished without the physical presence of the other twin. Emotionally immature Noushcka vacillates between displays of childishness and maturity.

As the children of an absentee father who is also a confirmed Separatist, both Noushcka and Nicholas have a strong interest in the political climate in Quebec. The fact that they have hardly ventured further than a few kilometers from their Boulevard Saint-Laurent neighbourhood helps explain their lack of perspective and their naivety. This aspect of their personalities reminded me of people I've met in the southern United States known as "crackers" who have often never set foot beyond fifteen miles of where they were born. These people have a rather peculiar and innocent lack of knowledge and understanding about how real life functions beyond the confines of their own small community.

The narrative of the book reminded me of two movies I rather enjoyed. In Blue Valentine with Michelle Williams and Ryan Gosling, the lead characters fall into the same destructive behavioural patterns as Noushcka and Nicholas. The same fate awaited Drew Barrymore's character in Riding in Cars With Boys.

The ending in The Girl Who Was Saturday Night caught me a bit off-guard but I'm not going to spoil it. You'll have to read it and draw your own conclusions. The book is a clever, well-written description of contemporary life in a small corner of Montreal.

Revealing secrets of the Paris Ritz Hotel

When I originally downloaded the book Hotel on Place Vendome I thought it was historical fiction but once I started reading I discovered it was non-fiction which pleased me even more. Written and thoroughly researched by Tilar J. Mazzeo, the book describes the opening of the world-famous hotel in Paris and its evolution from a modest, beautiful boutique hotel to the internationally-recognized institution it is today.

The main focus of the book centres on the years when it was occupied by the Germans during World War Two. Residents included Hermann Goering, who when he wasn't living a drug-addicted lavish life in the Imperial Suite spent his time looting Paris of its precious works of art. Coco Chanel shared digs with her German lover who was a high-ranking officer. After the war the couple fled to Austria where they lived for ten years until his death. Chanel was a permanent resident of the Ritz for most of her career. No satisfactory explanation has ever been given as to why Chanel did not suffer the same shameful fate as other collaborators.

As the liberation of Paris approached in the summer of 1944, the German occupiers fled with as much confiscated artwork and antiques as they could manage.

The allied forces who took over Paris included new occupants at the Ritz Hotel such as Ernest Hemmingway, Ingrid Bergman and Marlene Dietrich. Petty disagreements over lovers, ego and accomplishments resulted and do not speak well of the individuals involved. While I thoroughly enjoyed the book, I thought it could have offered much more information and insight than it did. For that reason I'm giving it seven out of ten.

Capital pays high interest

There's nothing more delicious than tucking into a really good book on a cool, cloudy afternoon. That's what I did today and finished reading John Lanchester's *Capital*, a book about the lives of a cross-section of Londoners faced with twenty-first century problems in their everyday lives. The book's title references money and how the high price of real estate in a London neighbourhood is a catalyst in each of the characters' lives.

The homes on Pepys Road which were affordable when they were built now command insane sums of money. The City stock trader has a lot of it and his wife enjoys spending it. The immigrant Pakistani family at the corner has considerably less, working long hours seven days a week running the local grocery store. A Polish builder is employing his physical skills and strong character to save for a better future. A rookie professional footballer gets a taste of it. A Hungarian nanny's ambitions are constantly challenged. An artist's grandmother who is one of the original owners of a home on the street when they were built dies. A Zimbabwian traffic warden's life as an illegal immigrant becomes entangled in the plot. Put all these fascinating characters into the pot, stir gently and a nice little plot as intriguing as Agatha Christie's "The Mousetrap" emerges.

The book has one hundred and seven short chapters which made me feel like I was making quick progress as I became increasingly more invested in the daily lives of each of the characters. The author intelligently and sensitively covers a number of issues including the death of a parent, greedy ambition, terrorism, parenting, love, ethics and the definition of success. When I read the last page late this afternoon I felt satisfied and happy. What more could you ask of a good book—a capital experience indeed.

Bad Monkey, good book

When a male friend suggested I read a book entitled Bad Monkey I was somewhat reluctant. Scanning the premise on the book jacket, it sounded like a guy's story. Hiaasen resides in Florida and has written a number of books located in various southern cities including Key West and Miami. As I began reading I became increasingly concerned that I was getting into a Miami Vice-type story but I was urged to push on and I'm sooooo glad I did.

Bad Monkey is a well-crafted, cleverly-written, funny story about a low-ranking police detective who suspects the discovery of a human arm on the end of a tourist's fishing line is a potential crime rather than a simple and unfortunate shark attack. The story includes dozens of colourful characters whose lives intertwine in surprising and interesting ways. While the monkey has a rather minor role he is part of a common thread that pulls everything together and he really is nasty.

In fact, I enjoyed the book so much I'm going to read more by this author. Fun, fast read. And I didn't even have to buy it. I downloaded it from the library. Bonus!

The Goldfinch deserves to be a bestseller

At almost eight hundred pages *The Goldfinch* by Donna Tartt requires a fair commitment time-wise but it's worth it. The title is the name of a rare seventeenth century painting by a Dutch master that is taken by Theo Decker a thirteen-year old boy when the museum in New York he is visiting is bombed, killing his mother. His low-life absentee father turns up and takes Theo to live with him in Las Vegas where he meets Boris, a young Russian immigrant in his class at school.-Boris has a similar chaotic home life. As life evolves they lose track of each other until they meet again ten years later in New York.

The story is engrossing and entertaining. One friend found it to be a bit tedious about half-way through but I rather enjoyed the level of detail and minutia. I'm always amazed at how authors come up with such plots and characters. The book is full of vivid descriptions of alcohol and drug-taking and leaves me wondering whether the author gained this knowledge through personal experience or thorough research. She also is knowledgeable about European art. Characters are clearly described with philosophical observations throughout the book and particularly at the end where she ties up the loose ends. The painting is treated like a live character. I can see why *The Goldfinch* is a best-seller.

Still Life with Breadcrumbs finally came to life

After being so totally entralled with Anna Quindlen's non-fiction Lots of Candles, Plenty of Cake I couldn't wait to read her latest fiction book, Still Life With Bread Crumbs.

The story centres around Rebecca Winter, a divorced sixty-year-old photographer whose work has made her a recognizable name over the years. The book's title is the title of her most famous photograph. As sales of her work diminish along with her bank account, she sublets her comfortable Manhattan apartment and moves to a furnished rural cabin with an absentee landlord. The outcome is a sort of re-birth for Rebecca.

I was fully half-way through the book before I finally got into it. The first half was a bit boring and I couldn't understand why it had become a best-seller. I attributed its success to riding on the coat-tails of her earlier books. Then, all of a sudden it picked up momentum and I was totally into it. I'm still not sure why it's best-seller-worthy but it is ultimately a good read and I'm glad I stuck it out.

Sue Monk Kidd scores again

Movies adapted from books rarely capture the nuances an author conveys with the written word. While the world enjoyed the movie, *The Best Exotic Marigold Hotel* with Judi Dench and a great cast of talented Brits, it paled in comparison to the original book *These Foolish Things* by Deborah Moggach. The book provided a lot more background on the quirky characters before they went to India and actually was funnier than the movie. If you haven't read it, I highly recommend it.

Similarly, I read the book *The Secret Life of Bees* by Sue Monk Kidd before I saw the movie and, again, the book was infinitely better.

I just finished reading her latest novel, *The Invention of Wings* and it was another winner that I couldn't put down. The book is historical fiction based on the lives of real-life sisters Sarah and Angelina Grimké who were early abolitionists and pro-feminists in Charleston, South Carolina in the early to mid-to-late nineteenth century. At the age of eleven, Sarah is given a birthday gift of a ten-year old slave girl called Hetty, also known as Handful. At a young age Sarah witnesses a slave being beaten and is so traumatized by the event she is temporarily rendered mute then develops life-long speech difficulties including sporadic stuttering. Her younger sister Angelina becomes her ally in her fight against slavery. The story follows the lives of several southern women and men in the Grimké circle. Sue Monk Kidd's books always have a spiritual element that drives her characters without being preachy. She provides fascinating insights into the lives of mid-nineteenth-century women in the south, juxtaposed with their counterparts in the northern states. *The Invention of Wings* would also make a good movie but could never capture the thoughts, motivations and subtleties so beautifully outlined in the book.

During the time I was reading this book, I also saw the movie, *Twelve Years a Slave*. That prompted me to dig out a book called *Within the Plantation Household – Black & White Women of the Old South* by Elizabeth Fox-Genovese which I purchased more than ten years ago after touring an old plantation near Charleston. It's a bit of a grim read – more like an academic work, but interesting nonetheless.

Now that I have three stories within one month about slavery behind me, I think I need to move on to something a bit lighter. Time to return to another P.J. O'Rourke or David Sedaris-type book.

Sheryl Sandberg says it like it is

As a retired businesswoman I couldn't wait to read Sheryl Sandberg's Lean In, the New York Times' best seller full of advice for working women. Sandberg joined Facebook as Chief Operating Officer in August 2013 after six years as Vice-President of Google Inc. I must admit up front that I approached the book with a bit of prejudice. I assumed she was a silver-spoon Type A über-achiever who expects other women to be as motivated and capable as she is. While the lady definitely had the advantage of starting out on second base, she knows what she's talking about in relation to gender issues in the workplace, office politics and the general dynamic surrounding working women. And she does not expect other women to be as ambitious as she is.

Although the book contains plenty of interesting anecdotal information to back her up, it is supported by an exceptionally large body of research. In fact, fully one-third of the volume of the book (I read it on my iPad) is a bibliography of resource and reference material. Her research skills (or those of her assistants) are indeed impressive, even tedious. While I was prepared to question the veracity of her observations, I found myself agreeing on most issues.

For example, Sandberg says:

1. "Fear is at the root of so many of the barriers that women face. Fear of not being liked. Fear of making the wrong choice. Fear of drawing negative attention. Fear of overreaching. Fear of being judged. Fear of failure. And the holy trinity of fear: the fear of being a bad mother/wife/daughter." I agree that our fear of failure or not measuring up often keeps us from taking risks, putting our name forward for a promotion, raise or new job. There is a shocking degree of mediocrity

among the male senior executives of many corporations while capable women sit on the sidelines lacking the confidence to go for it.

2. "One reason women avoid stretch assignments is that they worry too much about whether they currently have the skills they need for a new role. This can become a self-fulfilling prophecy, since so many abilities are acquired on the job. An internal report at Hewlett-Packard revealed that women only apply for open jobs if they think they meet one hundred percent of the criteria listed. Men apply if they think they meet sixty percent of the requirements." When I was appointed Marketing Manager I wasn't sure what the position even meant. It was a new position within the company so I had the opportunity to create and develop the job on my own. In the beginning I made up for my lack of experience with enthusiasm. One of the first things I did was make an appointment with The Globe and Mail to go down and meet with one of their business writers so they could "open a file" on our company. That resulted in a full spread about our firm on the front page of the business section. Quite a coup for a novice and gave me a solid running start. The flip side is naiveté. Many business women forge ahead and succeed because they don't know about or don't consider the possibility of failure, or do not consider the lack of experience being a problem.

Other more practical reasons women may avoid stretch assignments are because they simply do not have the extra hours in the day required to fulfill the demands.

3. "It's not only working parents who are looking for more hours in the day; people without children are also overworked, maybe to an even greater extent. When I was in business school, I attended Women in Consulting panel with three speakers: two married women with children and one single woman without children. After the married women spoke about how hard it is to balance their lives, the single woman interjected that she was tired of people not taking her need to have a life seriously. She felt that her colleagues were always rushing off to be with their families, leaving her to pick up the slack". Sheryl Sandberg is admittedly in the enviable position of being able to afford plenty of domestic help in the form of nannies and housekeepers to handle domestic issues. Not everyone has this advantage. I never had children

and often felt that with the hours I spent commuting and working in the office or traveling for business, there was simply no time left to throw children into the mix. It's easy to feel resentful when you're working your fanny off and colleagues in the office are working on their children's school projects. That's life and it's not always fair.

4. "I sometimes struggled to pass the "fitting in" test." She's not alone and describes smoking cigars and going on fishing trips as part of an effort to feel accepted. I recall attending an industry "stag night" with hundreds of construction professionals at a convention centre. I could easily have by-passed the event but wanted to attend on principle – to demonstrate that the industry was not for men only. There was only one other woman in attendance. To the best of my knowledge, that business association no longer has stag nights; they have another name for the event and a number of women in the business attend. I also once accompanied several male co-workers to a gentlemen's club (aka strip club) where my co-workers sat in the front row. I'm not sure what point I was trying to make that night but as one of the few female managers at my company, I guess I wanted to be seen as one of the boys – rightly or wrongly. I have since learned that such measures are not necessary or particularly appropriate.

Women bring a special dynamic to the management scene. We cannot all be Sheryl Sandberg's nor do we want to be. Her version of a stressful workplace/family conflict is discovering her daughter has head lice while flying to a corporate event in a private jet. Not easy to empathize or sympathize. She needs to suffer the stresses single working mothers or low-income women experience every day of their lives trying to do the best for themselves and their families while working full-time.

I do agree with her, however, that the incremental strides the women's movement has made for improving equality in the workplace should not be taken for granted or considered as less of a priority. Within the time-line of my own career I have seen things get better but there is still a lot of room for improvement. Whatever changes are made to better accommodate the work/life balance ultimately benefits both men and women. Maternity leave has been matched by paternity leave. While it may seem like equality on the surface, it's not perfect. Both men and women experience challenges returning to work, finding they've lost their place in line and have to scramble to make up for lost time.

Young parents today are not willing to make the sacrifices in their family lives they witnessed their own parents, the baby boomers making. Ultimately, while we want all working people to have a happy, balanced personal/work life, we also need businesses to succeed in order to sustain those jobs. The financial bottom lines are what keep businesses viable.

Lean In is certainly a controversial book and worth discussing. I enjoyed reading it and despite my earlier prejudices I'd give it a thumbs up!

Excellent read by Canadian author

What a pleasure it is to read a good book by a Canadian author. Road Ends by Mary Lawson is set near New Liskeard in northern Ontario and London, England in the years between 1966 and 1969. Road Ends chronicles the lives of various members of a small town family that includes seven boys and one girl. I could relate not only to the small town setting but also to the descriptions of Megan travelling to England in 1966 when she was twenty-one, as I also traveled to England in 1967 by myself at the age of twenty. Road Ends is a fast read covering a complex set of circumstances and personalities. I had to wait a few weeks for it to become available to download from my local library as it's a current best-seller but it was worth the wait. The book is well-written, engaging and a genuine page-turner – just what I like.

Who do you think you are?

Canada's own Alice Munro winning the Nobel Prize for Literature is just about the most exciting thing that could ever happen in the literary world. As Canadians, as women, as readers we're thrilled that she has been recognized on such a prestigious level. But the best part is that her writing celebrates simple, everyday life in southwestern Ontario.

I'm looking forward to going back and re-reading her stories, particularly "Who do you think you are?" In 1967 I actually had a male boss at Bell Canada say those very words to me. I had presented him with a summary of ten suggestions on how we could improve efficiency and work flow in the Cable Assignment office where I worked. He informed me that "There are people in other departments getting paid a lot more than you are to come up with solutions – who do you think you are?" That's when I stopped speaking to him altogether and went on to accomplish more in life and business than he ever could have hoped to. And I'm not alone. I have friends who also were also told "you aren't smart enough for university" and other similar put-downs. Alice understood this.

Alice doesn't live here anymore

Alice Munro is without doubt a very good author – after all she recently won the Nobel Prize for literature. The thing is – and I'm embarrassed to admit this – I just don't get her. I applauded her winning the Nobel Prize and was as proud as any Canadian could be. It motivated me to dig out my hard-cover copy of her latest book, *Dear Life* and give it another shot. About three-quarters of the way through the book I gave up – again. While her stories of the people and small town places in southwestern Ontario ring familiar, I find them tedious and depressing, which, as someone who grew up in a small Ontario town is understandable. But her story lines and writing style fail to make me want to turn the page and keep reading. If someone could explain why she was Nobel-worthy I'd be very grateful.

I'm just a simple lover of books, not a student of literature, an academic, a critic or probably even all that smart. So there's obviously something I'm missing. There are so many other Canadian authors I like better than Alice Munro which makes the criteria for selection from the world-wide pool of Nobel Prize contenders even more incomprehensible.

The answer I think lies in the subjectivity of the reader. I've also found that I rarely liked Oprah's book club picks either. Some were wonderful reads but for the most part they were bleak and depressing. Similarly, the Giller prize winners consistently leave me cold. I no longer go out and buy the latest Giller books because I'm always disappointed.

My most reliable source of recommended great reading material is my Boomer Broad friends. Our tastes are similar for the most part and when they're not, I simply stick with the ones I like. My tastes run to historical fiction, non-fiction, humour, biographies and autobiographies. No more Alice Munroe. No apologies.

Boomer broad meets Bridget Jones

A friend and I attended a fun event sponsored by *ELLE Canada* magazine and Girls Night Out Ontario wine to introduce Helen Fielding, author of *Bridget Jones's Diary* and *The Edge of Reason*. Both books were smash chick-lit hits followed by equally successful movies starring Reneé Zellwegger, Hugh Grant and Colin Firth.

A cocktail reception was held in The Burroughs Building at Queen Street West and Bathurst in downtown Toronto to celebrate the launch of *Mad About the Boy*, the final installment in the Bridget Jones trilogy. The venue, trendy raw loft space with exposed brick walls and an ancient elevator was once used for manufacturing furniture. In this hip atmosphere we felt quite Bridget Jonesey sipping wine and nibbling h'ors doeuvres and Purdy's chocolates with all the young and beautiful creatures – and me.

An interview with Helen Fielding was conducted by *ELLE Canada* followed by questions from the audience. Helen got married and has had children since publication of her original books about twenty years ago and it has only been within the last couple of years that she felt she was ready to take Bridget to the next step.

While Ms. Fielding admitted to many similarities with her main character, she was clear in stating that the books are works of fiction. Her experiences resonate so realistically with female readers because she writes in her own voice, "just like I'm writing a letter to a close friend" she said. She confessed to wearing her Spanx for the event in order to appear at her best which most women in the room could relate to.

At the end of the evening we went home with a signed hard copy of *Mad About The Boy*, along with a bottle of wine, some chocolates and goodies from Rimmel makeup. There's nothing better than a good hen party, unless of course it's a Vicars and Tarts party.

Only the strong survive – or do they?

I had just finished ordering Malcom Gladwell's new book, *David & Goliath* from Chapters on-line (taking advantage of a forty percent discount) when I decided to check out Geoff Smith's blog. Geoff is the President & CEO of my former alma mater, EllisDon Corporation and his blogs are always insightful and inspiring. Both Malcolm Gladwell and Geoff Smith have addressed a subject about which I have very strong feelings – that we are each masters of our own destiny and personal happiness and very often the Davids succeed while the Goliaths fail. I also referenced this in my review of Jeannette Walls' book, *The Glass Castle*.

Several months ago I watched a documentary on TV about half-a-dozen billionaires from around the world – how they made their fortunes and what made them different. In every case the individuals came from very humble beginnings. They had neither financial nor educational advantages. None were university-educated and they all came from poor families yet they built successful businesses.

What makes such people rise above difficulties while others do not is a subject that is endlessly fascinating to me and I am convinced that in order to succeed one has to have been *hungry*, metaphorically speaking. Getting ahead and succeeding in life by today's societal standards requires a certain kind of innate intelligence not necessarily associated with education, as well as a large dose of good old-fashioned grit and determination. Each of us alone is responsible for our own success. And once we have achieved this there is no room for complacency. Just ask Blackberry.

By the way, did you know that Malcolm Gladwell grew up here in Ontario, Canada (check him out on Wikipedia) and coincidently we share the same birthdate – albeit sixteen years apart. No wonder he's so clever.

Listen to Your Hormones

Watching Dr. Natasha Turner on The Marilyn Denis show (www.marilyn.ca) the other day reminded me that I have to pay more attention to what goes into my body. I'm convinced my itching, bitching and all-round BOOMERbroad falling apart issues are hormone related but it's hard to give them the attention they deserve. I've read about Natasha Turner in the past but last week's episode prompted me to go out the next day and purchase my very own hard copy that I could highlight and bookmark for reference. And when I read a book I like, I want all my friends to experience the same high, so I recommended they purchase it as well – or at least borrow it and read it. Now I've set myself up for a challenge.

Although I already consume a relatively healthy diet with little to no sugar or alcohol, I do drink tea, including green tea and unfortunately must admit that my one major vice is Diet Coke – preferably a large fountain Diet Coke, not the somewhat inferior canned or bottled kind. I keep my carbs to a minimum and always eat whole grain. I try to buy organic foods whenever possible and plan meals to be at least two-thirds veggies. Since I've been going to Weight Watchers – again (www.weightwatchers.ca) my go-to snack has been fruit so generally I've been a very good girl. Although I love sweets, I've sworn off most cookies and treats until I achieve my weight goal.

I'm now going through Dr. Turner's book with a yellow highlighter and a fistful of Post-It bookmarks. My intentions are good. Let's see how I do on the follow-through.

Elizabeth is Missing

For a debut novel, Emma Healey's Elizabeth is Missing is remarkable. The book combines understanding and empathy for dementia with mystery and suspense. Maud Horsham is in her eighties and while still living in her own home with the assistance of her daughter and a daily caregiver, she struggles with the challenges of memory loss and confusion associated with geriatric dementia. She writes copious sticky notes to herself which she stuffs into her pockets to prompt her memory while her caregiver and daughter leave similar notes stuck to walls and doors around the house to help Maud retain a sense of reality and perspective.

When Maud cannot contact her only remaining friend, Elizabeth, she enters a world of fear, confusion and frustration when no one takes her concerns seriously. She has stopped by Elizabeth's house, contacted Elizabeth's son, gone to the police and even placed an ad in the local paper to help locate her friend. This loss is tumbled in her brain with the loss of her beloved only sister Suki after World War Two, a disappearance that was never adequately explained.

The early half of the book was at times a bit slow as the reader wades through Maud's lengthy internal dialogues trying to make sense of her thoughts and actions. While I understand it is all part of setting the scene, I became frustrated at times with the lack of progress. This little stumble in my opinion is minor compared with the overall cleverness of the plot. It was a fast read and as it picked up momentum toward the end I couldn't put it down. I'd give it eight out of ten.

Facing my addictions

My name is Lynda and I am an addict. My preferred substance is even stronger than fountain Diet Coke and music from the sixties. There is no twelve-step programme and even if there were, I am not interested in rehabilitation. My problem has become particularly intense since I retired and now have the time to truly indulge myself.

I am a magazine junkie. I buy them, I read them, I hoard them and blow my money on them every chance I get. My pulse quickens when I encounter ancient magazines in doctors' offices, big fat fashion magazines in hair salons and salacious dog-eared gossip rags on the dirty coffee table where I get my car detailed. No sources are beneath my enjoyment. It started with a simple subscription to Chatelaine decades ago. That felt so good, I soon had to up the ante and ordered a Canadian decorating magazine, then another.

Despite subscribing to no less than eighteen monthly publications, I still want more and can justify them shamelessly. Magazines purchased at the grocery store are not magazines; they are groceries. I have scoured the internet trying to source out-of-date magazines at bargain basement prices. Reading month-old material doesn't bother me in the least (see "doctors' offices" above). Seeing out-of-date magazines being packed up in the drug store (an appropriate venue) for return to the publishers to make room for the next month's edition breaks my heart. Why won't they just let me take them home. I'd love them. I'd cherish them. I'd run my fingers lovingly over their beautiful, glossy coloured pages.

I spend some of the winter months in Florida which provides me with a U.S. address to further feed my addiction. And it's encouraged by pitiless American junkie publishers who are continually offering me "deals". My e-mail is frequently bombarded by tantalizing offers I cannot refuse. I'm immediately hooked on subscriptions for three magazines for a total of only fourteen dollars per year – for all *three*. How could I refuse offers of a one-year subscription for only five dollars!! That includes high-end glossy magazines that retail for six-fifty *per copy* at the newsstand! A few years ago, J.C. Penney offered me my selection of three magazines for a mere five dollars in total. And two of them are still coming.

I can now order my favourite British mags to read on my iPad for a fraction of what they cost at Chapters, and sooner than it takes for them to arrive in hard copy. And now, my local library also offers magazines available for downloading, the high-tech version of my drug dealer. The downside of reading them on my iIPad is that I can't rip pages out and file them. And unless I have a special printer from Apple, I can't print them either. Special highlighter pens with a cartridge of Post-Its in the barrel are always by my side. My magazines are riddled with skinny Post-Its flagging the pages I have marked for future reference. I buy those pens in bulk and have them planted all over the house.

Much as I try periodically to get a grip on my habit, it persists. Like the sirens' song, my magazines beckon. If the postal carrier doesn't produce at least one score in my mail box every day I get the shakes. And when there's a bonanza day with three or four, I can't wait to put the kettle on. Then I get out my high-lighter pens and go to work. I have a well-rehearsed system for reading them. The first run-through is to simply peruse the visuals – no reading of particular articles allowed at this stage. That's what the post-it flags are for. Later, during the second reading, I take my time and read each advertisement, every letter to the editor and every article, page by page. I rarely skip anything.

My girlfriends love my addiction. Every few weeks I purge my stash and pass the expunged copies along to friends who in turn pass them along to more friends. Before passing them on, I tear out highlighted pages for filing in a special blue toile case subdivided into such categories as Hair, Makeup, Clothes, Livingroom Furniture, Bedrooms, Kitchens, Paint Colours, and so on. Tearing out pages does tend to be a sore point for friends who complain about missing vital pages of an article they want to read that I've archived.

In my next life I want to be a magazine editor. Instead of writing letters to the editor after the fact, I would be like Anna Wintour in charge of getting my own way, with plenty of free product to boot. I get high just thinking about it. I only hope it leaves me enough time to devote to my other addiction – books! Oh – and purses. Don't get me started.

Imagining a better book club

As an avid reader I should probably belong to at least one book club, but I don't. The reason is that I simply love books too much to try reading one that's not a total delight. Book clubs provide wonderful social and intellectual opportunities for readers and I think they are incredibly valuable instruments for meeting people and enriching your mind. However, they're just not for me. While reading a book that's not of my choosing might expand my mind, it also shortens my life and becomes too much like homework. It reminds me of plodding through *Return of the Native* in high school. I could have been reading something I loved instead.

One of the first questions I ask people when I meet them is, "Do you read much?" and "What are you reading now?" I love to hear the answers as I frequently get excellent recommendations. And it's a great ice-breaker for interesting conversation. I could never understand the appeal of the book *"The Secret"* by Rhonda Byrne. It was predominately recycled information and hardly qualified as ground-breaking. So, when I heard there was a discussion about the book at a local bookstore, I decided to go and see what I was missing. Only two people showed up – me and another woman. Even the facilitator was M.I.A. The evening did turn out to be worthwhile however, as the other woman introduced me to *Wild Swans* by Jung Chang which turned out to be a marvelous book. And I gave her the names of some of my favourite Canadian authors. Fellow readers are always great company.

I have summarized pages of unread titles I can't wait to get at. I often read two or three books simultaneously while squeezing in time for my eighteen monthly magazine subscriptions. My library card gives me access to thousands of books – free – on my iPad. If I'm really desperate for a particular book, I can pay to download it on my Kindle.

And Amazon always has incredible deals on used books, often costing as little as one cent plus the cost of shipping.

The kind of book club I would like to belong to would be more of a "Show and Tell" affair. I would love to share a cup of tea or a glass of wine with fellow readers while we go around the room and have each person show and describe what they're currently reading. Each person would have a time limit for their oral presentation followed by a time-limited question period.

No matter how you access the written word, it's magic. I always love discussing books with other readers. I should probably organize a Book Sharing Group but I'm too busy reading and, truth be told, probably a bit too lazy. Retirement can sometimes do that to you.

Well-heeled means not wearing Manolo Blahniks

Pearl Bailey once said, "I've been rich and I've been poor and honey, rich is better." I know I've certainly been poor at times in my life and it was not fun. Not having money can mean living a simple, happy, uncomplicated life but in today's world it more often means worrying about not having enough to pay our bills, how to save for a home or vacations, or the big one, how to retire comfortably.

After hearing the young author interviewed on the radio, I just finished reading a book called Well-Heeled – The Smart Girl's Guide to Getting Rich by Alberta's Lesley-Anne Scorgie. Well-Heeled is one of the best books I've come across for providing practical advice for young twenty and thirty-something women about how to best manage their money.

When Boomers were growing up in the fifties and sixties, credit cards were not part of our vocabulary or our parents'. Visa and Mastercard did not exist so other than Diners' Club for traveling businessmen, everyone paid cash for everything they purchased. I clearly remember paying cash to my dentist in the late sixties (thirty-five dollars, which was half my weekly salary) when I went for checkups and cash to my doctor for piercing my ears (the old-fashioned way with a needle). We paid cash for shoes, clothes and gifts. Charge accounts at major department stores were available but of no use to anyone in our small town where there was no Eatons or Simpson's store. We did have mail order offices for Eatons and Simpsons but it was rare for anyone to use a credit card back then. Business was strictly cash.

As a result of not having the option of charging frivolous purchases to credit cards, we were perhaps more cautious with our pennies. Boomers started working full-time in the mid-sixties and when we saw a blouse we liked, we either had to go to the bank on our lunch hour and withdraw the cash from our savings account (and banks were only open between 10:00 a.m. and 3:00 p.m. back in the olden days) or write a cheque which involved the inconvenience of filling out a detailed information form and having it approved by the store manager. I remember once at the old Savette store at Dundas Street West and Roncesvalles purchasing a kitchen table. When I wrote a cheque for it they even took my picture for future reference.

I'm horrified as I watch Gail Vaz Oxlade's Til Debt Do Us Part show on television. The show often features young couples who, despite receiving sometimes tens of thousands of dollars in wedding gift money have managed to rack up ninety thousand dollars in consumer credit card debt. Did no one teach them about managing money? I think the more likely cause is that parents were always there to give these young people everything they wanted and bail them out when they ran into financial trouble. I finally had to quit watching the programme as I got too frustrated and depressed watching it. Financial troubles are a major cause of breakups among young couples. It is very important to not only be smart about money yourself but to make sure your partner is on the same page.

If young women would listen to only one piece of advice it would be to stress the importance of financial independence. And the simple reason is that having a nest egg means you have options. When I was in my fifties during the recession that lasted most of the 1990s, I was broke. It was difficult to find work and it was incredibly stressful because I had no financial resources to draw on. After reading Your

Money or Your Life by Vicki Robin I decided to give up self-employment and re-enter the corporate world. This would assure me of a regular paycheque, health benefits and a chance at building some retirement equity. It worked. But I wish I'd been more frugal in the seventies and eighties when I was blowing my hard-earned bucks on eight hundred dollar ultra-suede power suits and silk blouses. Being able to distinguish between needs and wants is an important first step. Scorgie outlines more steps young women can follow to achieve security.

Being a financially-savvy young woman is not only smart, it's sexy. The late Helen Gurley-Brown, former editor of Cosmopolitan magazine said that one of the reasons her husband David Brown (producer of such block-buster movies as Jaws) was attracted to her was because he appreciated that she had been smart enough to own her own (used) Mercedes that she'd paid cash for. When we're fifty years old and out of work or wanting a life-style change, the credit card debt we accrued buying that Coach handbag or "I-just-needed-to-get-away" trip to Cuba will be an enormous ball and chain around a young woman's ankle. In Scorgie's words, "If it's on your ass, it's not an asset!"

Financial security is really about freedom

In the course of reading Well-Heeled even this old Boomer learned a few things I didn't know, such as, you can arrange for your bank to automatically transfer the money out of your chequing account to your credit card on the same day you make the purchase on your credit card so you will have zero balance at the end of each month. That means you know exactly where you stand on a daily basis. I often get confused about my credit card balance as it's shown on my on-line statement and when it is due. They never seem to jibe. When I got my first credit card in the seventies, I diligently kept a running list on a piece of paper in my wallet, like a cheque book, of every purchase and the amount spent each time I used my credit card so I wouldn't have a heart attack when the bill arrived. Scorgie also provides several excellent website addresses for tracking, planning and saving tools such as Mint.com and bank websites. I plan to check out the one she recommends for calculating how much retirement income we'll need.

Lesley-Anne Scorgie is an excellent example of what can be accomplished by young women with smart financial planning. She has guested on Oprah and other television programs as a result of her personal successes. Well-Heeled is written to get young women started on the right foot or get them back on track if they've fallen off the rails. If you have a daughter or granddaughter or know a young woman who could benefit from learning how to better manage her money, please get on-line (Well-Heeled – The Smart Girl's Guide to Getting Rich) and send her this book. Everyone deserves to have the options and freedom that financial security can bring.

Chapter 10
Media

In The Year 2525
. . . Zager and Evans, 1969

More Geezer Pleasers Please

Last week my guy and I went to see The Grand Seduction, a light-weight movie about the efforts of the residents of a remote Newfoundland harbour community to attract a doctor. If they could land a doctor then they could convince investors to build a waste disposal facility to provide jobs for locals no longer employed in the fishing industry. As fans of Rick Mercer and *22 Minutes* on CBC and going back even further to CODCO, we both love Newfoundland humour—smart, sharp and usually deftly delivered. Although a bit corny, we enjoyed the movie even though we were the only people in the theatre.

It's getting harder to find movies that appeal to baby boomers. While we all enjoyed Quartet and The Best Exotic Marigold Hotel (based on an even better book called These Foolish Things by Deborah Moggach), movies that our demographic can enjoy are few and far between. Hollywood keeps pumping out action hero movies like Godzilla, X-Men, Transformers, Live, Die, Repeat targeted to the eighteen to thirty-five age group while a huge category of movie-goers called Baby Boomers are barely acknowledged by the so-called brains in the movie-making business. We may be geezers to them but who else has the financial wherewithal to drop fifty bucks on a pair of movie tickets and grossly over-priced popcorn and pop. We love going to the movies and there are millions and millions of us willing to spend our money at the theatre rather than illegally down-loading them.

Zoomer TV's weekly show on Vision network hosted by Denise Donlon alongside Conrad Black addressed exactly this issue. Wendy Crewson and Mary Walsh were panelists on the Zoomer show and as Boomer Broads they were able to contribute unique insights. I found Mary Walsh's off-hand comments about The Grand Seduction (in which she had a supporting role) particularly interesting because the whole time I watched the movie something didn't sit quite right with me and she nailed it. That movie, like most movies produced today was a totally male-dominated piece of work—directed, written by and starring men. Wonderful men for sure but the female characters were totally skewed to a misogynistic stereotype. As Mary Walsh pointed out, the leading male characters completely ignored the fact that strong women are actually the community leaders and initiators of community-building projects in these rural areas. By casting the women in The Grand Seduction as eavesdropping telephone operators and witless seamstresses whipping up white cricket outfits for their men, the movie missed a huge opportunity to let the women's voices be heard through the genius of actor/writers like Mary Walsh to make the movie far better than it was.

The list of movies currently in theatres leaves me cold. I can totally do without monsters, space aliens, vampires, endless car chases, gratuitous violence, annihilation, and anything with Tom Cruise. Just in case someone with a bit of influence might read this, here are a few suggestions on what we Boomer geezers would like to see in movies:

- Comedies – A good laugh is always uplifting.
- Romance – Who doesn't enjoy a bit of sentiment. It gives us hope.
- Foreign locations – We love to visit foreign locales like Paris, Rome or London for the price of a movie ticket.
- Contemporary themes – When the plot centers around people our age we can relate.
- History – Whether fiction or fact, we always enjoy nostalgia.
- Character study – Getting involved in the lives of complex characters is satisfying and makes for good conversation afterward.

A movie like Monuments Men could have been so much better if the writing had not been so trite and cliché. Philomena was wonderful for all kinds of reasons. Clint Eastwood's Grand Torino is a quiet gem. We loved Bridesmaids for its sharp wit, great physical comedy and intelligent writing. Ditto for The Full Monty. And Dallas Buyers' Club was just a damn good movie.

Do you get the picture? Please answer our call.

Vacancy at the Grand Budapest Hotel

Maybe it was all the hype beforehand that set me up for a bit of a disappointment. While I enjoyed *The Grand Budapest Hotel* movie, I can't say I loved it.

The movie is a fantasy piece set pre-World War Two about the lives of lobby boy Zero Moustafa (Tony Revolori) and the concièrge M. Gustav (Ralph Fiennes) at a wedding-cake-type old hotel located in the mountains of an obscure European country. The narrator describes how the hotel's ownership came to be through a series of stunning visual sequences and physical comedy that reminded me of early Peter Sellers movies. The plot centres on a disputable will left by a murdered wealthy guest played by Tilda Swinton. I'm a big Swinton fan and would have liked to see more of her character. The sets were stunningly detailed and I wondered how much of it was filmed in a real hotel that time forgot.

Cameo performances by such well-known names as Owen Wilson, Bill Murray, Ed Norton Jr., Harvey Keitel, Jeff Goldblum, Willem Dafoe, Jude Law and others were fun to watch. The writing was brilliantly funny and with intelligent use of irony (one of the writers is British) which meant plenty of belly laughs. Thinking about the movie afterward, I somehow thought it is more of children's fairy tale that could have been equally well done as an animated film. But then, I'm just someone who likes to go to the movies and perhaps this one needs to be viewed and appreciated by someone more erudite than I am. Nonetheless, it was fun to watch.

The Dallas Buyers Club Effect

Last night I finally watched the Oscar-winning *Dallas Buyers Club* with Matthew McConaughey, not realizing until the credits at the end that it is based on a true story. Set in 1984, the movie details a time in the life of Ron Woodroof, a hard-living homophobic Texas electrician and rodeo buff whose rough and careless lifestyle lands him in the hospital where he is informed he has AIDS/H.I.V. and is given thirty days to live. When conventional medicine fails him, he resorts to back-alley alternative treatments which result in moderate improvements to his condition. He begins to educate himself about the disease and launches into an all-out effort to provide himself and other victims with the seemingly simple but unavailable treatment drugs. He reluctantly befriends a transgendered drug addict who becomes his business partner and together they launch a dispensary in a motel room to provide victims with the drugs they need to stay alive.

The movie grabbed me emotionally right from the beginning with my early discomfort soon turning into anger and frustration. What struck me as ridiculous obstacles to treatment in 1984 are not all that different thirty years later? My anger is precipitated by the seemingly total control that the pharmaceutical industry has over doctors, hospitals, medical care and the governing food and drug authorities. While I am certainly no expert on the treatment of chronic diseases, as a simple bystander I am troubled by the questions raised. Why is it that after two generations of charitable organizations raising billions of dollars for cancer research and treatment, some progress has admittedly been made but not proportionate to the time and dollars being thrown at the problem.

In my humble, boomer-on-the-street opinion it is not in the best interests of the pharmaceutical industry to come up with a cure for cancer. Imagine if we had directed those billions of dollars instead into the science of cause and prevention. There is evidence that stress is a significant factor in the cause of chronic diseases. Is there a correlation between the incidence of cancer and the chemicals in our food chain, specifically the use of pesticides and food genetically modified to withstand large doses of chemical pesticides? We may never know because research is controlled by the large pharmaceutical and chemical companies complicit with the federal control agencies.

We all know someone who has lost a friend or relative to cancer and some with AIDS. We seem to be making a snail's progress on cures. Is it time to start standing up to the big guys and demanding answers that do not amount to pat-on-the-head rhetoric encouraging us to be patient? Let's start looking further down the line at what chemicals are doing to our environment and what we put into our bodies.

Case in point: the recent removal from Subway sandwiches of a chemical called azodicarbonamide used for aeration in such plastic products as shoe soles and yoga mats (http://abcnews.go.com/Health/subway-takes-chemical-sandwich-bread-protest/story?id=22373414) and the announcement by Kraft Foods Inc. that they will be removing dangerous yellow dye from three of their mac and cheese products for children. I guess the rest of us don't merit that attention. Every day we blithely pour quantities of azodicarbonamide, which has been banned in Europe and Australia, into our bodies in hundreds of foods. Perhaps we should step back and take a closer look at these types of additives as potential causes of chronic diseases. But we need the food industry, the chemical and pharmaceutical industries and governing authorities to be responsible and honest about the danger associated with these products and that's not going to happen.

Thank you *Dallas Buyers Club* for reminding me to be vigilant about what I consume and to not accept what the large multi-nationals are saying is the truth and to demand the truth they are keeping from us. It makes me sick.

Boomer women and Monuments Men

History was certainly not my favourite subject in school, which in retrospect I think was largely due to the quality of the teacher we had. History as it was taught in the sixties was largely something to be memorized and regurgitated on an exam with no understanding of the human side. As an adult I now have an almost insatiable interest in days and people gone by. My husband I are both huge fans of the History channel and other channels that show documentaries of world wars, ancient civilizations and everything in between. We have a trip to France planned to visit the historical sites of Canadian battles in both the first and second world wars including Juno Beach, Dieppe, Vimy, Ypres, The Somme and other sites. Perhaps this interest stems from having a grandmother who was a war bride from England in the First World War and a very special now-deceased family friend who fought in horrific conditions as a sixteen-year old at The Somme. Many relatives are also veterans including an uncle who was a prisoner of war captured in Hong Kong in 1941 and held by the Japanese for four years.

Naturally, I was looking forward to seeing The Monuments Men at movie theatres – and not just because it stars George Clooney—that was simply a bonus. It's the story of a small group of art specialists tasked with locating upwards of half a million works of art stolen by the Nazis from private collections, museums and churches across Europe and returning them to their proper owners. The movie is based on a true story and scenes in the movie accurately depict old black and white photos of actual events. For that reason, I thoroughly enjoyed it. The one shortcoming I found, however, was the fact that the dialogue was very often trite and cliché. I think such a fascinating subject could have been handled with more intelligence and depth. There were also brief moments of comedy which relieved the serious depiction of war.

Overall, I'd give it three out of five based on unrealized potential but I'm not an expert. But, do go see it. *The Monuments Men* is a good movie.

P.S. Here's a link for those who are interested in learning more about the real story behind the movie http://www.smithsonianmag.com/history/true-story-monuments-men-180949569/#.UwT9TO5uJX0.email

But is she Oscar worthy

Last week a friend and I went to see *American Hustle*. The bushel of theatre popcorn was wonderful – warm with just the right amount of salt and crunch. The gallon of icey Diet Coke I slurped from the holder in the arm of my chair was perfection. The seats were very comfortable.

And the movie was a lot of fun with plenty of plot twists that had me guessing who were the good guys and who were the bad guys. The trickery reminded me a lot of *The Sting* with Robert Redford and Paul Newman many years ago. I definitely think it is worthy of an Academy Award nomination for its clever script and all the other factors that generate the more boring awards. I do have a problem; however, with Amy Adams being nominated for Best Actress in a leading role for delivering what seemed to me to be the worst fake English accent ever. Or maybe it was intended to sound fake. Is that good acting or bad acting? It certainly hurt my ears every time she employed it. The chemistry between her and Bradley Cooper was intense and palpable but how much acting does that require? Who wouldn't melt when getting up close to Bradley Cooper! And Jennifer Lawrence was incredible as the wife of Christian Bale's character. Two thumbs up from this Boomer Broad.

A familiar scenario with a twist

My friend Terry and I went to see Judi Dench in Philomena. I must admit, based on the trailers I saw on television, I was expecting a mildly interesting film about a common occurrence, something perhaps more appropriate for a made-for-TV movie. Philomena, a young Irish girl has a baby out-of-wedlock in the 1950s. She is given over to nuns in a convent for the duration of her pregnancy and the delivery of the baby. In return for their "charity" Philomena is indentured to the convent for four years after the birth during which time her little boy is given for adoption.

The movie reveals Philomena's fifty years of silence about the birth and her final search for the little boy she lost. While I'm not going to give away the plot and twists, I will say that we were both surprised and uplifted by the quality and intelligence of the film. We should have known that anything with Judi Dench would not disappoint and Steve Coogan's subtle performance was perfect. *Philomena* is based on a true story so check it out while you can. Hope you enjoy it too.

And So It Goes

Diane Keaton is one of my favourite celebrities for a variety of reasons, the main one being her authenticity. (I once was amazed to find myself sharing an elevator with her at the old Four Seasons Hotel on Avenue Road in Toronto on my way to our company Christmas party.) I never miss attending her new movies as soon as they're released. She's had a few clunkers for sure but *Annie Hall* was her zenith. I've watched that movie so many times I can almost recite the dialogue from start to finish. Sadly, her latest movie *And So It Goes* co-starring Michael Douglas is, in my opinion, a clunker. Keaton's movie characters always tend to be a variation of herself with her insecurities, unfulfilled ambitions and a wardrobe of soft cashmere sweaters, turtlenecks and tailored blouses. And with Rob Reiner as producer and also playing a minor role in the movie I expected better.

And So It Goes is the story of a sleazy real estate agent played by Michael Douglas who was recently widowed and is selling his own multi-million dollar family home. He temporarily moves into a tired-looking rental unit in a waterside four-plex he owns until his own home sells and he's ready to move on to Vermont. Keaton plays a widow who lives in the adjoining unit. Douglas' estranged, now-clean formerly-addicted son turns up unexpectedly with a ten-year old daughter and wants Douglas' character (who didn't even know he had a granddaughter) to look after her while the son does a bit of jail time. Grumpiness ensues for Douglas followed by romance and ultimately a predictable happy ending. The dialogue was trite; the premise a bit silly and all in all not worthy of Keaton, Douglas or Reiner. Try harder next time, guys. We know you can do better.

Dear John: I love you

John's Doyle's regular column in *The Globe and Mail* is always an interesting read. Despite my cranky relationship with TV service providers, I genuinely enjoy watching television—well, certain programs anyway. I despise the usurious rates charged by the cable, internet and satellite companies which cost more per month than heat and hydro for my home and rank far lower on the scale of necessary utilities.

Back to my buddy John Doyle, the *Globe's* TV critic. We seem to be like-minded in our television tastes and opinions. I don't like reality shows. I love PBS which fortunately is free. I do enjoy Canada's basic networks like CBC, Global, CTV and CITY but I hate that we can't live-stream their news programs when we're visiting in the United States. (I've been e-mailing everyone on the planet about this issue for years, to no avail.) I also love HBO, the History Channel and even the Military Channel with its excellent documentaries. And I'm going to miss Stephen Colbert not being Stephen Colbert any more.

According to Doyle it's just as well I missed Seth Meyers' interview with Lena Dunham. I'm a huge fan of Dunham because she's so (and I hate to use this overworked word) *authentic*. She's also incredibly smart, creative and energetic and I'm surprised she didn't stomp all over Meyers.

John Doyle laments the inattention paid by the TV media to white males of a certain age. Do the program decision-makers actually make use of market studies? Why is it that the eighteen to forty-five demographic is still targeted as the Holy Grail? Their market research must date from 1971. Boomers are a much larger slice of the pie and we probably have more money to spend on the drugs, step-in bathtubs, vacations and incontinence products touted by their advertisers. Therefore, we deserve to be catered to and listened to—white males *and* females, crones, codgers and boomers alike.

Back to my beefs with the cable and satellite sharks. I've tried by-passing the service providers by watching via my laptop but that's not yet a perfect system. A friend gave up on cable years ago and relies on rabbit ears with a fair level of success. But the only way to get HBO and other programs I like is to send Bell Xpressview a gigantic slice of my pension and a pound of my wizened old flesh every month. I'm watching with interest to see what happens with Amazon getting into the movie and TV show rental business.

I'm keeping my fingers crossed that the current proposal is passed by the government to force service providers to unbundle television channels. Consumers deserve a break and being allowed to pick what programs we are willing to pay for should be a given. Although I'm confident even then they'll screw us by charging more for what we want. I currently pay about twenty-five dollars per month to PVR programs that are on too late at night or that I'm not home to watch. In the U.S., much as I have my list of beefs with Comcast, I can call up any missed program *free* on channel one or three hundred. I asked Bell about whether they had that option the other day when I was talking to them about another issue and the guy didn't know what I was talking about. Nothing is free here – not even choice. All I'm asking for is the ability to watch what I want, when I want and to pay accordingly for those choices.

And in closing, John, I feel so validated to think that you share my opinions. Obviously you're very smart.

Reserved seating on Boardwalk Empire

"What shall we do? What *shall* we do?" asks Dr. Narcisse on an episode of *Boardwalk Empire*.

At the suggestion of a couple of girlfriends who started watching HBO's *Boardwalk Empire* series, I decided to check it out on HBO-On-Demand and immediately became addicted. Having just finished watching *forty-eight hours* (not consecutively) encompassing four seasons, I thought by the forty-eighth episode I would know what they did. Instead, I'm left wondering what they're going to do next.

The *Boardwalk Empire* storyline is based on real-life mobster characters in 1920 prohibition-era Atlantic City, Chicago, New York and Philadelphia. Many of the behind-the-scenes players also worked on The Sopranos including Martin Scorcese, Terence Winter, Mark Wahlberg, Tim Van Patten, Lawrence Konner, Howard Korder and Margaret Nagle. The result is an earthy, graphic depiction of the lives of such colourful characters as Nucky Thompson, Al Capone, Lucky Luciano, Myer Lansky and many others.

If you liked The Sopranos, you'll love *Boardwalk Empire*. There's plenty of sex, booze, drugs, violence, corruption, politics and gripping story lines based loosely on historical events as they happened in the era of Prohibition. While watching the series, I was struck by two things:

1. Business is business. Whether it's legitimate or illegal, there's a pronounced hierarchy with everyone's job description clearly defined and compensation is not always fairly administered. A lot of time and effort is spent in meetings negotiating for power and trading territories for profit. Just like in today's business world, it's a constant pissing match.

2. Being a bad guy is very stressful. Watching the daily lives of each of the characters reminded me that no matter what job we have in this world, life's not always fair and the good guy does not always win. While bad guys make their share of inroads it comes at a terrible price. Imagine looking over your shoulder every minute of every day looking out for someone to "eliminate" you? There's an unbelievable amount of job stress associated with killing, stealing and being a bad guy or gal. Think I'll stay squarely where I am in my life choices—on the *right* side of the law.

Most of the actors in the series are not particularly familiar faces and not beautiful or handsome by Hollywood standards. Teeth are crooked and bodies are not perfect. Interestingly, authenticity was so accurate that even the bare boobs seem to be real ones not surgically enhanced – i.e. they're not always huge and not always pert (that alone should get my male readers to watch). And the producers have kept the characters and plots moving through interesting and sometimes shocking changes that are not always sympathetic. The costumes are amazing. Photography is exquisite. The acting is delightful. Tune in on HBO.

TV or not TV – that is the question

My relationship with my television satellite supplier is a love/hate thing. Most of the time I hate them for the usurious monthly rates they charge – more than I pay for heat and hydro which provide a more valuable service. However, after years of resisting, I finally caved in a couple of years ago and ordered HBO and PVR. Some of the programming on HBO is of such good quality that I've become a bit of a nuisance in trying to convince friends to subscribe so I can talk to them about the programs I like to watch.

In addition to Bill Maher, Broadchurch and a number of other programs, I'm a great fan of *Girls*. Twenty-seven-year old Lena Dunham is absolutely brilliant (and I don't use that word very often) as one of four New-York single girls coping with everyday life. She's an author, screen-writer, actor, producer, director – you name it – she's done it. While the writing, dialogue, plots and characters in the show are masterful, it's Dunham's physical presence that continually commands my admiration. She's not your typical tall, thin-with-big-plastic-breasts blonde, toothy version of young womanhood so prevalent in the media today. Dunham is a real, unaltered, natural and intelligent human being who should be held up as a role model for young women today instead of the above-described Barbie-doll types. Her figure is not perfect; her teeth are not the oversized wall-to-wall bright white veneers flashed by everyone else on TV; her hair is brunette and does not appear to involve complex extensions and hours of work in the chair; her makeup is usually minimal with none of those fool-the-camera makeup tricks; and in the character of Hanna, her clothes are unspectacular and often unflattering. Her voice is feminine without the baby-doll inflection common in young women's speech patterns. In short, she looks and sounds like most of the human race and I love her for it.

I've also started watching and really enjoying *Getting On*, a show about a group of geriatric patients in a California extended care facility, and their quirky care-giving staff. Based on an original BBC series created by comedienne Jo Brand, *Getting On* is a dark comedy, again with excellent writing and a killer cast. One of the things I like most about this show is the realistic cast of actors including Laurie Metcalf who played Roseanne's sister, as the tightly-wound Dr. Jenna James, an angst-ridden doctor who is not entirely happy in her line of work as she feels she has a higher calling. The three nurses played by Alex Borstein, Niecy Nash and Mel Rodriguez are perfect caricatures of any nurses you would encounter when visiting your own relative in a similar facility. The humour is dark and at times unbelievable but that's the essence of its appeal. I heard the producers being interviewed on Sirius satellite radio and they had genuine concerns about being able to find actors who actually looked old in the land of over-the-top plastic surgery. They brought many older actors out of retirement for the show and the results are wonderful. One of the patients, Birdie Lamb, is played by Ann Guilbert who used to play Laura Petrie's neighbour Millie Helper in the old *Dick van Dyke Show* in the sixties. Again, minimal to no makeup, people who look and talk like real human beings and scenarios that are a ton of fun to watch.

The flexibility of television viewing now has evolved to the point that we can truly watch what we want, when we want. With PVR, Netflix, On-Demand, internet streaming and other options available, we can pretty much craft our TV watching to eliminate the crap we don't want. Hopefully, before long that will include eliminating the extortionist rates charged by our service providers. That's something I'd really like to see.

Broadcasting live from Canada
Not in my backyard

More than three million Canadians spend the winter months in Florida contributing in excess of four *billion dollars* annually to local economies. It seems we're still considered suspect, however, because Canadian television news is something the U.S. satellite and cable service providers will not provide. In Canada, we get NBC, CBS, ABC, Fox, CNN – you name it – all the American news channels are available through our local satellite, internet and cable services. But the reverse is not possible in the United States.

I've contacted Comcast in Florida on numerous occasions only to be ignored. I've contacted the CRTC (Canadian Radio and Television Commission), individual television stations and networks and I keep running up against a brick wall called something like, "It's against regulations." Is Canadian content something to be feared? Are American service providers afraid of its citizens hearing another point of view?

I've tried various on-line programs to access real-time Canadian news programs and they're all blocked by Comcast. We'd even be willing to pay a premium for direct feeds from CBC (Canadian Broadcasting Corporation), CTV, Global or CITY TV. All we want to do is watch the snow plows on Highway 400 north of Toronto – it makes us appreciate our Florida homes even more.

I remember campaigns on TV in the fifties and sixties soliciting support for "Radio-Free Europe" to enable iron curtain countries to access western media. Here we are in 2014 soon to be 2015 and we need a campaign to allow Canadians to access real-time Canadian TV live in the United States. Access is available to BBC and other foreign countries, even Al Jazeera but not CBC. Surely this is fixable. Is anyone listening who can help?

There's something about Mary

Mary Walsh is one of my favourite people in the media. I recently had the pleasure of hearing her speak at the Bluma Appel Theatre in the Toronto Reference Library. The library has an ongoing program of speakers and events that are enormously interesting and they're free. Interviewed by *Toronto Star*'s Richard Ouzounian, Mary reminisced about her childhood, her start in the entertainment business and over the course of an hour related experiences in a conversational format. She's currently starring in a one-woman show entitled *Dancing With Rage* which despite Richard Ouzouian's less-than-kind review is no doubt worth the price of admission.

Strong women always inspire me. Mary Walsh rose above a difficult childhood, alcoholism, an abusive relationship, macular degeneration and many professional failures to become a Canadian icon. A chronic under-achiever in school, she revealed that she got a total mark of seven in her high school French exam. When compared with my own mark of fifteen, I'm an absolute genius.

I remember enjoying her along with Cathy Jones, Greg Malone, Andy Jones, Tommy Sexton and the rest of the cast many years ago on *CODCO* from Halifax and of course, more recently *This Hour Has 22 Minutes*. Mary and Cathy's *Friday Night Girls* from *CODCO* still make me smile when I think of them. Presenting herself to Toronto Mayor Rob Ford in her Princess Warrior character resulted in an unprecedented call by his Lordship to 911, a defense never before taken by any other politician. And she's challenged them all.

Mary's wonderful Newfoundland sense of humour and her natural intelligence combine to make her a wonderful writer, actor and social commentator. My dream would be to write and observe life from her perspective. In the meantime, I'll just wait, watch and listen for more Mary Walsh.

I'm sick sick sick of the KKK's

Writers have always been advised and encouraged to write about what they know. Today, I've chosen to ignore that advice in order to vent about something I know very little about. Would someone please tell me what is so newsworthy about the Kardashian klan—Kris, Kim, Khloe, Kourtney, Kendall, Kylie—the whole kkk-koven? As part of my research and to be fair to the perpetrators I decided to watch an episode of *Keeping Up With The Kardashians* on TV but that only added anger to my state of bewilderment. After ten minutes I couldn't take any more and switched channels. Sitting at the head of the table was an old surgically altered woman who goes by the name of Bruce Jenner who may or may not be in a lesbian relationship with Mama Kris. Mama K blessed the whole family and thanked the God of Greed and Great Glorification for her incredible good fortune and the invention of money and plastic surgery.

The rest of the show treated viewers to scenes of entitled, spoiled, insensitive family members whining about other entitled, spoiled, insensitive family members. All this was carried out while sitting aboard a massive yacht anchored somewhere exotic. Perhaps using the word *insensitive* is unfair. After all, people who do that much name-calling and bitching about their first-world woes must have a level of sensitivity that is higher and far more developed than my own. Otherwise, how could they claim any level of unhappiness living in a world that delivers them every material reward conceivable without actually having to work for it.

Papa K, who passed away in 2003 was best bud, assistant legal counsel and supporter of O.J. Simpson. The kids come from fine stock indeed. In fact, it's rumoured that one of the little K's (Kourtney?) was even fathered by Simpson. Credentials don't come much better than that. The Jenner klan at one time also had their own reality series when Jenner spawn Brody and Brandon were the stars of *The Princes of Malibu*. At that time, Brody and Brandon's mother Linda Thompson (ex-girlfriend of Elvis Presley) was married to our very own Canadian music producer David Foster who was step-fathering the spoiled Jenner boys. I also tried watching that but didn't have the intestinal fortitude. Fortunately, Foster finally saw the light and dumped the ex-Mrs. Jenner. Whew!

I should have probably used some sort of genealogical flow chart to explain the icky interrelationships in the KKK Klan but that would give them more legitimacy than they deserve. Who is financing these people and their lavish lifestyle? Marlene Arpe had a choice K-quote from Kendall in the *Sunday Star*, "I want to be taken seriously. People think that this (success) just came to me. But it didn't." Arpe's, "I made the call to Mommy all by myself" says it all. It's a made-in-America phenomenon that is a sad commentary on the state of the union. I'd like to think it just wouldn't be korrect here. It's not very Kanadian, eh!

Shame on Zoomer magazine

When I opened my mailbox one day (the old-fashioned kind – at the front of my house) I went nuts. There on the cover of one of my favourite Canadian magazines, the April 2014 edition of *Zoomer* was the picture of Andie MacDowell, an American celebrity who has no place getting this kind of print space in an intelligent publication for and about people associated with the **Canadian** Association of Retired People. In a country of thirty-five million fascinating people, could Zoomer not find a single interesting Canadian to feature? How about me? I'm also "smokin' haute at sixty-six"!

The accompanying article, "earth angel" references the Canadian connection as being MacDowell's role in Cedar Cove, a Hallmark adaptation of American Debbie Macomber's book series of the same name that was filmed in Vancouver—a somewhat tenuous connection to justify the space. Putting celebrities on the covers of magazines like Zoomer and my favourite women's publication, MORE always annoys me to no end. Both mags are a cut above the usual print fare and I am disappointed when they go for the cheap shot. Celebrities like Andie MacDowell are perfect for gossip publications like People or Us or any number of other American celebrity rags but not Zoomer, despite the fact she's fifty-six years old. I'm disappointed, angry and insulted that they would stoop to such cheap tactics as the picture of a common American celebrity to attract buyers on the newsstand. Shame on you. There are thousands of more interesting personalities I would prefer to see profiled.

As a snowbird, we find it impossible to get news about Canada and Canadians when we are in the United States. The American media is totally focused on what goes on only within the U.S. borders. The rest of the world is incidental – unless its politics involve the United States. I've actually met people in Florida who had no idea where Toronto is. It's hard to believe that in this shrinking world full of amazing, exciting and interesting characters, there is still so much focus on American celebrities. And if anyone shares my feelings, make yourself heard.

Footnote: I sent a version of this posting to *Zoomer*'s blog and they actually published it in the comments section. Here's the link: http://www.everythingzoomer.com/behind-cover-andie-macdowell-april-2014/#.UxpM84V2je1

To "e" or not to "e", that is the question

Digital e-readers are becoming increasingly more popular and are available in different devices to suit most individual preferences and pocketbooks. A divide does exist, however, between those who have embraced the new technology and those who prefer the traditional hard or soft-cover paper version. I have one foot firmly planted in each camp. On one hand, I love the convenience of downloading books from a retailer or the library from the comfort of my LaZ-Girl chair with a lovely cup of tea at my side. On the other hand, I'm a dedicated fan of cracking open a wonderful new book, the old-fashioned kind with ink imprinted on paper. I admit to sometimes even bringing the paper version up to my face so I can smell the wonderful musty aroma. Older books have a very special warm-sunny-day-sitting-in-a-chair-by-the window dusty smell that only enhances the reading experience.

Over the past few years I've acquired four e-reading devices and I'm still not satisfied that I've achieved e-reader nirvana. Here's an outline of the steps in my quest for the ultimate, perfect device:

My first e-reader was a rather hefty and expensive (at the time) Kindle that I purchased shortly after they launched. I incorrectly concluded that bigger and more expensive would be better and would minimize the obsolescence factor. I found that first Kindle to be too big and heavy and passed it along to a grandson.

The smaller, pocket-book-sized Kindle proved to be perfect for toting along in my purse but because of Amazon's proprietary software I couldn't download library books. Back to the mall.

The next and most expensive step was to purchase an iPad so I could add e-mail capabilities, colour screen, durability, reputation and web-searching benefits to my list of performance enhancers. I loved being able to carry it around for web-browsing and e-mailing but before long, I again found it too big and heavy for everyday reading. Start the car! (Unlike a trip to IKEA, this quest is costing a lot of money.)

The Kobo seemed like the next logical step. Available at Chapters/Indigo, they had several models with various features and a wide range of price points. Previous experience with my first Kindle and iPad told me that bigger and most expensive was not necessarily the best way to go, so I opted for the Kobo Touch which is their least expensive version. I'm embarrassed to say that I still have not achieved e-reader perfection. My new little Kobo is a joy to carry around as it's light as a feather and takes up hardly any room in my purse but it's a bit hard to read in low light, such as reading in bed with poor lighting.

Looking back at my checkered past in e-reader experimentation, I now think I should have purchased an iPad mini or similar Kobo device with internet, colour and web-browsing capabilities in the first place. These devices will never replace my laptop for word processing but they definitely have value and are a joy to use. My second little Kindle would have been perfect except I'm now a colour-screen snob and I like to download from the library and my little Kindle can't accommodate that.

In the meantime, I've pre-ordered an old-fashioned hardcover copy of Ken Follett's *Edge of Eternity*, Book Three of the Century Trilogy. At more than eleven hundred pages, that should keep me busy for a while and keep my mind off the tempting virtues of an iPad mini. I absolutely can't wait to dig into Edge of Eternity and by the time I finish I should have steroid-worthy biceps and snoot full of lovely paper and ink smells. By then it should be Christmas.

And to all a good night . . .

If I were ol' Santa, you know what I'd do
I'd dump silly gifts that are given to you
And deliver some things just inside your front door
Things you have lost, but treasured before. I'd give you back all your maidenly vigour,
And to go along with it, a neat tiny figure.
Then restore the old color that once graced your hair
Before rinses and bleaches took residence there. I'd bring back the shape with which you were gifted
So things now suspended need not be uplifted.
I'd draw in your tummy and smooth down your back
Till you'd be a dream in those tight-fitting slacks. I'd remove all your wrinkles and leave only one chin
So you wouldn't spend hours rubbing grease on your skin.
You'd never have flashes or queer dizzy spells,
And you wouldn't hear noises like ringing of bells. No sore aching feet and no corns on your toes,
No searching for spectacles when they're right on your nose.
Not a shot would you take in your arm, hip or fanny,
From a doctor who thinks you're a nervous old granny.
You'd never have a headache, so no pills would you take.
And no heating pad needed since your muscles won't ache.
Yes, if I were Santa, you'd never look stupid,

You'd be a cute little chick with the romance of a cupid.
I'd give a lift to your heart
when those wolves start to whistle,
And the joys of your heart would be light as a thistle.
But alas! I'm not Santa. I'm simply just me,
The "matronest" of matrons you ever did see.
I wish I could tell you all the symptoms I've got,
But I'm due at my doctor's for an estrogen shot.
Even though we've grown older, this wish is sincere,
Merry Christmas to you and a Happy New Year.

While we can all enjoy the humour in these thoughts, is there one of us who would trade where we are today for what we were forty years ago? This Boomer thinks each day is even better than the day before and I would never really want to go back. We're blessed; we're beautiful; we're Boomer Broads. Thanks for reading. And I look forward to the upcoming year being the most wonderful year for all of us.

About Me

Born in 1947, I'm what you would call a Beta Boomer – one of the early ones. As first-borns, we were treated a bit differently from those who followed. Parents were stricter with us; we towed the line for a while. Then, we started to challenge the status quo – question dress codes, morals, music and expectations in life. The effect the Boomers had on the world, from mini-skirts and sexual revolution to where we are today has been profound. Now we're starting to retire, unleashing an entirely new interpretation of what that means. No sitting with our knitting for us. And our version of Grandpa smoking his pipe is rather different from earlier generations.

After forty years in the corporate world I retired to become a happy blogger, voracious reader and overall enjoyer of life. During my working life which began at age eight when I was still in school, I had many jobs including waitress, carhop, yarn spinner (yes – literally), taxi dispatcher, secretary, cable assigner, diaper deliverer, executive assistant and even go-go dancer for a couple of weeks. The majority of my career was spent as Corporate Marketing Manager for EllisDon Corporation, Canada's second-largest construction company completing more than two billion dollars in new construction annually by the time I retired.

My mental meanderings are primarily aimed at Boomer women to expound on how we turned out and what we think about the journey. It's also an opportunity to share some of the wisdom I've acquired over the years. Since I started blogging, however, I've noticed BOOMERBROADcast (aka Lynda's soapbox) appeals not only to women of all ages but men as well. Hope you like it as much as I love doing it. Let's rock n' roll.

Lynda Davis
For my blog, go to: www.boomerbroadcast.net
To order BOOMERBROADcast: www.amazon.com

Made in the USA
Lexington, KY
10 December 2014